SWORDS & DAGGERS

FRONTISPIECE A fine example of an early
17th century rapier with a long Solingen-
made blade. A series of gracefully curved
bars form the guard for the hand and a
heavy pommel balances the blade.

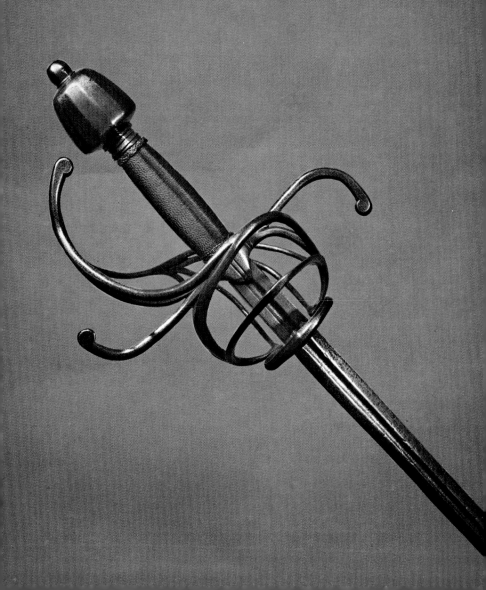

SWORDS &
DAGGERS

by
Frederick Wilkinson

WARD LOCK & CO. LIMITED
London and Melbourne

To Howard Blackmore and Claude Blair

© Frederick Wilkinson 1967

Printed in Great Britain by Richard Clay (The Chaucer Press), Ltd.,
Bungay, Suffolk
Set in Ehrhardt Monotype series 453 and 573

CONTENTS

Acknowledgements

I gladly acknowledge my very real debt to so many collectors who have helped me in every way, freely giving information and, in the case of those whose names appear below, lending choice items from their collections, often at some considerable personal inconvenience.

Special thanks are due to A. V. Norman, who read the manuscript with such good humour; G. Mungeam, who made many helpful suggestions; and, not least, to Ted Holmes, who took such trouble with the photographs.

Both I and my publisher wish to express our thanks to the following for their permission to reproduce photographs:

L. Archer 114, 117 (R), 145; G. Bennett 123 (L), 138 (L), 143, 144; H. Blackmore 72, 73, 183, 189; F. Bubear 8, 9; Collectors Arms Antiques Ltd. 120, 133, 135, 140, 142, 166; A. Dove 39, 65 (3); L. Gibson 42, 43, 53, 54, 80, 81; R. Gregory 141, 158, 159, 160, 165, 169, 187, 188, 190, 191, 192, 193 (R), 194, 195; D. Cyngell, Frontispiece, 38, 49, 50, 52, 56, 59 (R), 67, 79, 90 (L), 105 (R); W. Howarth 51, 55, 62, 64, 66, 68, 78, 83, 91, 97, 99, 100, 101, 102, 103, 137; G. Kellam 92, 93, 98 (I), 123 (R), 124, 131, 138 (R); A. Miller 30, 57, 65 (1, 4, 5), 69, 74, 75, 76, 89, 90, 98, 104, 108, 109, 110, 116, 117 (L), 121, 127 (R), 129, 130, 134, 136, 139, 146, 161, 162, 175 (R), 180, 193 (L); G. Mungeam 1, 2, 3, 4, 5, 7, 16, 31, 58 (R), 61, 82, 85, 86, 95, 96, 105 (R), 111, 118 (R), 125, 131; Penrose Collection 168, 170, 171, 172, 173, 174, 176, 177, 178, 179, 181, 182, 185; E. Perry 10, 58 (L), 65 (2), 71, 88, 106, 107, 112, 118 (L), 122, 186; A. V. Smith 44, 45, 46, 48, 70, 77; F. Stephens 149–156; T. Stubbs 147, 148; E. Valentine 21, 24, 29; A. Wade 41; Wallace Collection 17, 18, 19, 20, 23, 25, 26, 27, 28, 32, 33, 35, 36, 37, 47, 60, 87 (Reproduced by permission of the Trustees of the Wallace Collection).

INTRODUCTION

DURING the last two or three decades there has been an enormous increase in the number of people collecting antiques and this is especially so for those with an interest in arms and armour. Whatever the reason for this increase, and many suggestions have been made ranging from sheer escapism to status seeking, it is a fact that prior to the Second World War antique weapons were the choice of only a few discriminating collectors. Their number was small and the plentiful supply of weapons was quite sufficient to meet all demands, consequently prices were low and collectors were able to be very selective in their choice of specimens. After 1945 there came this great upsurge in interest, particularly in firearms, which naturally stimulated research, and many excellent books covering all aspects of firearms collecting were published. Newly available knowledge stimulated further interest, so increasing the demand, and this rising demand, coupled with a diminishing supply, brought about a steep rise in the price of antique firearms. Commercial interests soon realised the possibilities and began providing well-made replicas of many famous weapons together with powder flasks, bullet moulds and other accessories.

Strangely enough there was, at first, nothing like the same upsurge of interest in armour and edged weapons, but as soaring prices made it extremely difficult for the small collector to acquire antique firearms there was a gradual switching of interest. Armour, quite apart from rarity, presents certain display and storage problems, so that it was to swords and daggers that many collectors turned. Already this increasing demand is beginning to make itself felt, but as yet the effect on prices of commonplace items has been only slight.

What then has this increasingly popular type of antique to offer the collector? Lethal weapons may appear as a peculiar choice except for those with a vicarious pleasure in violence but, in fact, collectors seldom, if ever, consider the purpose of the weapons and by and large they are a very mild and respectable group. Any well-designed object has an aesthetic appeal which can be divorced from its *raison d'être* and however much one may deplore the purpose for which the weapons were intended it cannot be denied that the great majority have a grace and beauty of their own. In addition to this aesthetic appeal it must be agreed that there is also a certain romantic association and very few people can resist the opportunity to handle a genuine sword or dagger.

There is a certain similarity between the cultural evolution of Europe and the development of the sword from the simple, rather brutal, slashing weapon of the 11th century to the flamboyant rapier of the 17th century, then the light, effeminate, but deadly small-sword of the 18th century and finally the carefully planned, technically conceived cavalry sword of 1908. Within the wide range there are weapons to suit every taste; simple clean-lined regulation-issue swords; intricate metal tracery on a cup-hilted rapier or *schiavona*; massive two-handed swords; inlaid and enamelled small-swords. For the collector with a taste for the exotic there are jade-hilted daggers from India and Persia; curiously fashioned daggers from Africa or magnificently simple swords from Japan. Collectors can specialise in types of swords, weapons of a country, continent or century, or simply seek out specimens of a multitude of patterns that please. To all these attractions must be added those of price and availability, for it is still very possible to find pieces of reasonable quality at prices that are within the range of most collectors' pockets.

Introduction

Collectors will find that there is a dearth of readily available books on the subject and it is not always easy to identify specimens with certainty. This difficulty adds both a frustration and an excitement and tends to stimulate a more serious and enquiring approach to the subject. As research continues so further information becomes available and more lines of enquiry are inaugurated, and so the corpus of knowledge constantly increases.

A volume of this size cannot hope to do more than present a basic minimum of knowledge and offer suggestions as to sources of information, but it is hoped that collectors will find the material of use in pursuing a fascinating pastime.

PLATE 1 Illustration for a version of Vergil, printed in Strasbourg in 1502. The weapons and armour are, of course, contemporary in style. ▶

THE STORY OF EDGED WEAPONS

THERE are still too many gaps and uncertainties for a complete and detailed history to be written and it is not always easy to discern a clear line of development. Many weapons appear to have certain national characteristics, but even these are blurred by the fact that fashions were copied and thus a sword with an apparently typical German look may, in fact, have been made in England. Dating too must always be general rather than specific, for many swords continued in use long after a new style had been introduced, and indeed not only were they in use but were still in production. If any general trend can be said to exist it is probably a growing tendency to make greater use of the point and less of the edge, but even this very general statement has to be qualified with many reservations.

The history of the sword has been largely influenced by its manner of use: it may be intended primarily for thrusting, in which case, length of blade, rigidity and the point are of prime importance, but if it is intended for slashing, the edge is then of prime concern. Most swords have in fact been cut and thrust in that they could be used for both purposes, but in this case some compromise, as far as design is concerned, had to be effected. Again, the shape and size of the sword depended on whether it was for infantry or cavalry, and although it was generally discarded as an infantry weapon during the 18th century the cavalry continued to use it until they were, in turn, themselves made obsolete. Even at the end of its useful life controversy still raged as to whether the best cavalry sword was a slashing or a stabbing weapon.

Although not the oldest of weapons swords have been used since at least 3000 B.C., and if flint is included then edged weapons go back to man's earliest history. As with so many things the beginning of metal-edged weapons may be traced to Egypt, for the earliest paintings and sculptures show several types of swords, daggers and axes in use. Double-edged, straight-bladed swords, with a simple, narrow-waisted grip appear as the weapons of the mercenaries whilst many native Egyptians are shown using a sickle-like sword known as a *khopesh*. A number of contemporary native African weapons bear a striking resemblance in detail to these and other Egyptian weapons, but whether this argues an unbroken line of development or is merely coincidence is open to debate.

During the Bronze Age some swords had long thin blades and were obviously for stabbing, but the more common leaf sword was double edged and primarily a slashing sword. Iron Age weapons were basically the same as those of an earlier period and Greek vase decorations illustrate several types. Some were straight and double edged whilst others were double curved with the cutting edge on the inside of the curve in the same way as the later *kukri* of the Ghurka.

Greek swords were primarily slashing weapons, but the *gladius* of the Roman Legionary differed in that it was short and intended for stabbing. For long hours the recruit practised on padded posts set up in the barracks and one of his instructor's favourite dicta was that "two inches in the right place was sufficient". Short and wide bladed, the *gladius* was fitted with a hilt of bronze, ivory or alabaster and was carried on the right side since its short length enabled it to be drawn easily from that position. For his other offensive weapon the legionary carried one or two long-shafted, wooden-hafted javelins or throwing spears, and these were normally thrown early in the battle. Since the shaft was fashioned of fairly soft iron, when the point pierced a shield the weight of the wooden grip caused it to bend, so making it difficult to withdraw, and it thus hampered the efficient use of the shield and also prevented it being thrown back at the Romans. As cavalry began to play a more important part in the Roman army a larger, double-edged, slashing sword, the *spatha*, was increasingly used. Romans seem to have had little use for axes, unlike their enemies the Franks who made great use of small axes hafted for throwing.

Saxon and Viking swords were basically the same in design and detail but they are not common, for the great majority of grave burials lack swords although most have spears or the smaller knife weapon called a *seax*, *sax* or *scramasax*. These weapons range in length from six to 30 inches, but all are single edged with an acutely sloping point and they were obviously intended as a general purpose knife as well as a slashing weapon and were carried in a sheath suspended from a waist belt. Some of these weapons are finely inlaid with many styles and forms of decoration. Surviving swords are most frequently straight bladed, double edged, 30 to 40 inches in length and with little or no point, clearly indicating that they were primarily slashing weapons. Most of these and later swords have one or more grooves cut into the blade and these are often erroneously described as blood gutters, but they are in fact known as fullers after a groove cutting tool. They were intended to lighten the blade by removing some of the metal without sacrificing its rigidity and are found on sword blades of all periods. Scarcity of grave swords may mean that they were not commonly used by the majority of warriors, but it is more likely that they were too highly regarded as weapons for them to be wasted by being buried.

In order to balance the blade and make it easier to wield the sword a counterbalance was fitted at the opposite end of the grip and this is known as the pommel. Early pommels were often just flat metal washers, but soon acquired a certain decorative quality with such detail as animals' heads. From about the 9th century the pommel was often made with the top edge divided into an odd number of lobes, but this style was out of favour by the 11th century. Protection to the hand was afforded by a simple bar across the top of the blade—the quillons—which projected beyond the edge or shoulder of the blade.

PLATE 2   Head of a *francisca* or throwing-axe, very
popular with the ancient Franks. Mounted on a short
wooden shaft, this weapon was used with effect against
the Romans during the Gallic Wars. Axes with the same
shape continued in use until well into the 12th century.
Length of head $6\frac{1}{5}$ inches. French, 6th or 7th century.

The Normans who invaded England with William in 1066 were largely armed with a sword very similar to that of their Viking ancestors, although the quillons were rather larger and projected further out over the shoulder of the blade. Their pommels were of two main varieties—a brazil-nut shape, which was to remain in fashion until the latter part of the 13th century, and a roughly semi-circular or recumbent D-shape, which was to be discarded by the middle of the 12th century.

About this same period a new shape of pommel became common, although it is known to have been used occasionally at least a century previously, and this round, wheel-pommel was to continue in use, with variations in detail, until the middle of the 15th century. At first it was flat, but at the turn of the century the edges were shaved back and by the middle of the century it had acquired two hub-like projections at the centre, but this style was discarded and by the middle of the 15th century a solid, flat-sided disc was in vogue. Although pommels were usually of metal, weapons of the highest quality were occasionally fitted with ones made of jasper and other mineral compounds.

Blades were gradually increased in length and towards the end of the 13th century sword lengths ranged from 45 to 55 inches, but at the same time blades were made narrower, often with inlaid inscriptions in brass or silver. Not only was the blade increased in length but the grip was correspondingly lengthened so that in normal use the weapon could be used in one hand, but there was room to grasp the hilt with both hands to deliver a far more powerful blow. Collectors refer to this intermediate size as a hand-and-a-half, or bastard, sword. As the grip was lengthened so too were the quillons, and although the great majority were still quite straight some were made which curved slightly towards the blade. This tendency to curve the quillons increased until, by the middle of the 15th century, the great majority had very pronounced downward curves.

Improved body defences with stronger mail and extra reinforcing plates were making it extremely difficult for a sword cut to inflict any serious damage and there was a growing emphasis on the use of the point for stabbing. It was easier to inflict a wound by jabbing at the less well-protected parts of the body such as arm pits or groins than by slashing at those areas covered by armour.

Apart from the emphasised points, blades altered but little except in one respect and this change was occasioned by a variation in use, for it was becoming common practice to improve the grip on the sword by hooking the forefinger over one of the quillons. Thus, by the middle of the 14th century, some blades were made with the few inches of the edge situated just below the quillons left blunt and unsharpened, but this *ricasso* does not become really common until the 16th century. Following the appearance of the *ricasso* it was logical to add some form of protection for the finger and a small, hook-like bar was added below the quillon or, more rarely, the blade was actually shaped to accommodate the finger. Around the middle of the 15th century a similar ring was added on the other side of the blade and these two extra guards were known as the arms of the hilt.

During the 15th century the *estoc* was to become a very popular weapon. This was rather more of a short lance than a sword, for the blade was triangular or square in section and the weapon was designed solely for thrusting. *Estocs* were seldom used as the prime weapon except in foot combat at the lists, but books of the 15th century intended to instruct in all styles of combat, *Fechtbucher*, show how a combatant should use this type of weapon.

Two developments were taking place, probably in Italy, that were to affect the design of both hilt and blade in a most dramatic fashion. Sometime around 1480 one of the quillons was curved up towards the pommel to form a guard for the hand-knuckle bow, and at about the same period lugs on the quillons were extended until they united and formed a horizontal ring on the side. The hand was thus becoming enclosed within a series of protective loops and bars, and during the 16th century this tendency developed enormously. It has been pointed out that the improved armour had emphasised the need to thrust rather than slash and in Italy during the early part of the 16th century there was developed a style of

PLATE 3 This is a fine example of the knife-dagger known as a *scramasax* which was in common use from the 5th to the 10th century. Sizes varied greatly, ranging from a small dagger to a short sword. They were carried in a sheath at the belt. Length of blade 10½ inches. Saxon, 9th or 10th century.

sword play which was known as fencing. Masters set up schools to teach this new fashion in sword play which stressed not only the use of the point, but the use of the whole sword for defence as well as offence.

Fencing weapons were, at first, very long bladed, up to 5 feet in extreme cases, double edged with a short grip and a guard of loops and bars of varying complexity. This type, known as a rapier, first appears about 1530 and was probably of Spanish origin. Pommels on these weapons, indeed on the vast majority of swords from the 16th century onwards, were round or egg shaped. As rapiers were essentially civilian weapons they were consequently often of extremely fine quality and embellished with many forms of decoration —a few were even fitted with gold or enamelled hilts. About 1580 it became the fashion to cut or chisel the steel into high relief figures or patterns and much of this work is outstandingly good. German craftsmen who produced such weapons of superlative quality were Otto Wetter and two brothers, Daniel and Emmanuel Sadeler, all of whom worked in Munich.

PLATES 4 and 5   Illustrations from Mr. Angelo's *The School of Fencing with a General Explanation of the Principal Attitudes and Positions peculiar to the Art* (1787). Here we see "The guard of the sword and

Many of the fencing masters taught systems of sword play which required the use of an auxiliary item such as a glove with the palm covered in mail so that an opponent's blade might be grasped or thrust aside. Others favoured the use of a cloak wrapped around the free arm which was then used as a shield, but most popular of all was a dagger held in the left hand which was then used to parry an opponent's blade. From an early date in the 16th century special daggers were designed for this form of fencing and were often supplied with the rapier and decorated in the same style. Such daggers from Spain usually had a large shellguard springing from the quillons and narrowing towards the pommel, and a long, fairly thin, blade which had, just below the quillons, a recess to accommodate the ball of the thumb. Other left-hand daggers were simpler with a shorter blade and a defensive ring set on one side of the quillon block. This style of fencing with sword and dagger was soon out of fashion except in Spain where it lingered on until well into the 18th century.

Military swords were far less elaborate than the civilian rapier,

lantern opposed by the sword and cloak", and "The defensive guard of the small-sword against the broad-sword".

having much simpler guards which lacked the intricate combination of bars and arms. Simple cross-like guards had gone out of style by the middle of the 16th century and in the latter part of the 16th century most swords had rings mounted on one or both sides of the quillons whilst others had solid shells. Quillons were also curved to greater or lesser degrees.

Early in the 17th century another style of fencing was developed in France which made use of a shorter, lighter blade, although the guard with its bars and loops had become even more complex. As early as the 1570's many swordsmiths were replacing the very complicated loops and bars with simpler but more effective metal shells. By the 1620's these had become, especially in Northern Europe, large and bowl shaped and swords in this style, common during the Thirty Years War, are known as Pappenheimers after Gottfried Heinrich Pappenheimer, a noted commander who was killed in 1632.

The complete antithesis of the light, flickering rapiers were the great two-handed swords which flourished during the 16th century, although they were mentioned as early as the middle of the 14th century. Especially popular in Northern Europe they were used entirely as slashing weapons, being whirled round above the head. Most measure about six feet in length and weigh around eight pounds each—less than their size might lead one to expect. Many had that section of the blade below the quillons covered with leather and this enabled the user to grip the blade here and so effectively shorten the length of the weapon. Two hook-like lugs which project from the side of the blade just below this leather-covered section act as quillons to guard the user's hand. Large two-handed swords were popular in Scotland and were known as great swords, *Claidheamh mor*, from which is derived the term Claymore. These rare weapons have straight, down-sloping quillons which usually terminate in pierced trefoils. Claymores of the 17th century commonly have a single shell on one side of the quillons.

Long swords were frequently used as ceremonial or state weapons by royalty and those towns anxious to enhance their prestige, and this practise can be traced back at least to the middle of the 14th century. York, in England, possesses one such civic sword which once belonged to Sigismund, Emperor of Hungary and Bohemia. It had hung over his stall of the Garter in Windsor and after his death in 1437 passed, by way of a certain cleric's hands, into the possession of the city.

During the 17th and 18th centuries frequent wars stimulated an increase in the number of swords produced and also the types available. Ever changing tactics stimulated ideas about sword design and similarly new fencing styles were evolved which required different kinds of swords. It is during the second quarter of the 17th century that one very distinctive sword, the cup-hilt rapier, first appears and although it originated in Spain or Italy it was soon adopted in many other countries. Elaborate bars, guards, counter-guards and shells were replaced by one fairly deep rounded dish, often pierced or chiselled, with very long, thin quillons and knuckle-bow. This type of sword remained popular in Spain until the latter part of the 18th century although in other parts of Europe it was discarded much earlier. Blades are usually very long and thin.

Somewhat similar in general appearance, although easily distinguished, is the dish rapier of the mid-17th century for the dish is far smaller and less deep than on Spanish weapons and there is no knucklebow.

In France during this period the fencing fashion required a shorter blade and by about 1630 a transitional rapier with two shells, no knucklebow and two arms, was in use. This was the probable forerunner of a weapon that was to remain popular for the next century or so—the small-sword. By the last quarter of the 17th century the small-sword had acquired its basic form with a blade of around 30 inches in length, two small flat shells, a knuckle-bow, rear quillon often curved horizontally and an ovoid or urn-shaped pommel. Earlier specimens retain a simple, rather attenuated forward quillon. Two arms of the hilt spring from the quillon block and curve to meet the shells.

Delicate hilts of chiselled steel, gold, silver and brass were made

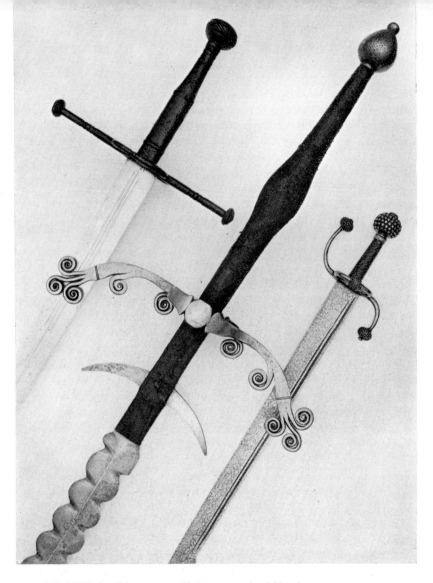

PLATE 6   The great differences in hilt sizes are
clearly shown by these three mid-16th-century swords.
On the left is a hand-and-a-half hilt measuring $7\frac{1}{4}$ inches,
the giant two-hander in the centre measures 16 inches,
and on the right the more normal single grip measures
a mere $3\frac{3}{10}$ inches.

and were sometimes further embellished with enamel plaques. Styles naturally changed during its century or so of use, but one useful general guide in dating is the size of the arms of the hilt, for these tend to become smaller as the 18th century progresses. During the first few decades they are large enough to be of practical use, but by about 1760–65 they have become so reduced as to be no more than decorative. Shells are a further guide to dating as early small-swords have them of equal size, and as the period progresses the inner was reduced in size. Finally the late swords have a single disc guard whilst military swords acquired a single boat-shaped guard.

Blades in a variety of shapes were produced, but they may be divided into three main groups—the ordinary flat, oval section blade, the hollow ground triangular section blade, and finally the *colichemarde*. This latter type is immediately recognisable by its thick top, or forte, of the blade which narrows sharply, at a point roughly a third of the length of the blade, to a very much thinner section, tapering off to the point. Designed to give strength at the top for parrying an opponent's blade, it still allowed easy, quick use of the point.

Small-swords were worn supported on two chains of differing lengths suspended from a steel hook which was slipped over a belt or waist band. Two spring clips engaged with the rings attached to metal bands on the scabbard which was usually of leather or parchment-covered wood.

Another weapon, very typical of the 17th and 18th centuries, was the hanger or hunting sword, for both terms are very often applied indiscriminately to the same weapon. These weapons are usually short and light with a blade of around 20 inches in length, fitted to a very simple hilt comprising a single knucklebow, short down-curving rear quillon and a high percentage have a small shell, or scallop, projecting from one side of the quillons. The metal parts of the hilt may be of brass, silver or steel and are frequently decorated with mythological or hunting motifs. Grips are of staghorn, wood or veneered with horn or tortoiseshell. Blades are almost invariably single edged, but may be curved or straight—as a working generalisation it may be said that the later ones are far more often straight. Similarly, brass-hilted hangers were primarily military weapons.

Another type of sword which flourished during this same period was the basket-hilted sword, although its early history is not at all clear. Germany was the probable country of origin and the earliest recorded forms appear around the middle of the 16th century. A great majority of styles are described as basket hilts, but their common feature is a cage of bars which cover the hand when holding the hilt. This cage may be formed by a few fairly wide bars or else by a complex interweaving of narrower metal strips. During the English Civil Wars of 1642–48 both Royalists and Roundheads favoured a cavalry sword with a straight blade and a fairly simple metal basket. Many of these baskets were decorated with embossed heads which were taken to represent the executed King Charles I, and for this reason they are often described as mortuary swords. In fact swords pre-dating the king's execution in 1649 bear these decorative heads. Probably the best known of all the basket hilts is the Scottish broadsword, known for many years as the claymore. Technically this title is incorrect since the true claymore was a large two-handed sword, but common practice has firmly established the term in general use. Many military units used swords which were very similar in shape to the claymore and the blades are always straight, although some are double edged while others are known as back edged or single edged.

Another group immediately recognisable are the *schiavona*, for their elaborate baskets are often very florid whilst the pommels, frequently of brass, are of characteristic shape. Some pommels bear embossed lions' heads since the weapons belonged to the Dalmatian mercenaries in the employ of Venice.

Increased mechanisation during the 18th century hastened a process which had started much earlier, that is, the growing emphasis on standardisation of military equipment. During the 17th and 18th centuries commanding officers had almost complete discretion in the manner of arming their units, but this freedom was

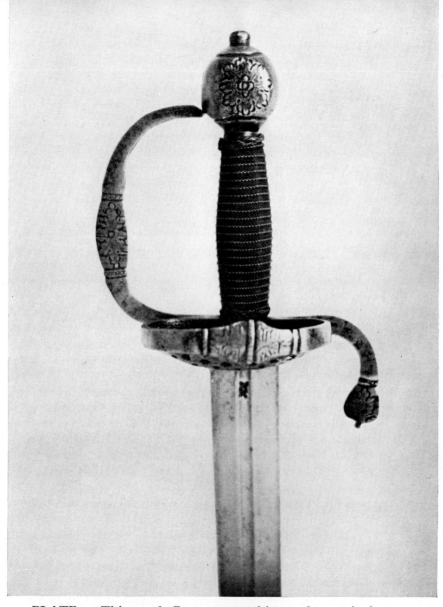

PLATE 7   This north German sword is another typical
example of a horseman's sword of the period. The grip
is bound with iron and copper wire and the pommel,
knuckleguard and single quillon all bear simple
decorations. There is a maker's mark on the blade.
Overall length 41 inches. Blade 35¼ inches. German, circa
1640.

gradually diminished and regulations were issued setting out details of the appropriate swords. In fact many officers placed varying constructions on the regulations so that absolute standardisation was not to be obtained for some time. British infantrymen carried a sword until 1786 when they were officially withdrawn, although some Scottish regiments were exempted from the order. Officers, of course, continued to carry swords and most of these were in the general style of a small-sword with a fairly light blade. In 1796 an order was made setting out details of these swords: a hilt of gilt brass with a straight blade, although this might be single or double edged. Heavy cavalry swords were also defined as being straight bladed, unlike those of the light cavalry who used a broad-bladed sabre with a simple stirrup hilt. It was at this same period that the steel scabbard first appeared in general use in Britain.

In 1822 another innovation appeared in the form of the so-called Gothic hilt, which is a simple half basket, and it is this style which has survived to the present. Many slight variations and adaptions have taken place during this long period, but they are too numerous to be listed here.

Swords are still carried by the officers of most of the world's armed forces, but they are, generally speaking, ceremonial rather than serious weapons. Apart from comparatively isolated instances swords were rendered obsolete by the First World War and infantry officers abandoned them as so much extra weight. Cavalry units continued to carry them until much later, but modern weapons had made this entire service old fashioned and useless. It was only in 1908 that, after extensive tests, a committee approved what was considered by many to be the best cavalry sword ever designed.

Although the sword was discarded by the British infantry in the middle of the 18th century, troops still carried their bayonets and this edged weapon still survives today. The name bayonet derives from the town of Bayonne in the extreme south-west of France, although originally the word was applied only to a type of knife. A well established tradition states that the idea of a bayonet was born when a group of combatants, having discharged their muskets, rammed the hilts of their knives into the barrel so enabling them to use the otherwise useless weapon as a spear for thrusting. Be that as it may, the idea of such a weapon as a military device appears to be of French origin and dates from the early part of the 17th century. Other countries adopted the idea—there is a mention of British bayonets in 1663—and by the early 18th century bayonets were general issue for most of the troops of Europe.

Bayonets of the 17th century were of the type known as plug bayonets since they simply pushed into the musket barrel. They had a plain, turned wooden grip which, apart from a bulbous swelling near the quillons, tapered slightly to fit firmly into the barrel. Quillons, often of brass, were quite short and the broad, double edged blade tapered gradually to the point. Although this form of bayonet was discarded in most of Europe by the beginning of the 17th century it persisted in Spain for another hundred years. Plug bayonets converted the empty musket into a short pike, but once in position it meant that the musket could not be loaded and military designers sought means to overcome this serious drawback. The first step was to affix rings to the hilt and these slipped over the barrel so securing the bayonet yet leaving the barrel free for loading and firing. By the end of the 17th century the French had evolved a far more efficient system whereby the blade was fitted to a short tube which slipped over the barrel and was held in place by engaging with a lug on the barrel. Socket bayonets like these were to remain in general use until around the middle of the 19th century.

Socket bayonets had long, stiff, narrow, tapering blades, which limited their use to that of a thrusting weapon. Attempts were soon being made to produce a bayonet which could also be used as a sword, and in Britain one of the first of such weapons was the brass-hilted bayonet for the Baker rifle, issued to certain regiments of the army around 1800. An enormous variety of socket bayonets was produced all over the world, some with wide blades, some with narrow and some with rings which locked the weapon into place to prevent them being wrenched off in combat.

Around the middle of the 19th century there was an increasing change from the socket fixing to that used on such weapons as the Baker bayonet. A slit was cut into the grip and this engaged with a lug on the barrel and when the bayonet was pushed into position a spring-clip locked it firmly into place. This system is still in use on most of the military weapons today. About the same time there was a fashion for bayonets based on the curved sword of the East, in particular the *yataghan* with its double curve. Other bayonets intended for the artillery or pioneers were given a saw back with the idea of providing a tool as well as a weapon. Every new military musket and rifle that was produced—and there were many—had its own special bayonet, and as there were often several models it will be realised that the number of different patterns is quite considerable and identification not always easy.

Unlike the bayonet the dagger has really never been a predominantly military weapon although it is, of course, historically much older with its beginnings in the flint hand-axes of the Stone Age. By definition a dagger is essentially a weapon with a tapering double-edged blade, whilst a knife has, again by definition, only one sharpened edge, but in fact it is often not easy to be precise when describing certain specimens. As a military weapon a dagger does not appear until the middle of the 13th century, but obviously most soldiers had carried some kind of small edged weapon from earliest times. Changes in style were fewer than with swords and at any given period several types might well be in use. Thus a soldier of the 14th century might have carried any one of perhaps four common types. There are many contemporary references to a dagger called an anlace, but its precise appearance is uncertain although it seems likely that it had a long thin blade and was essentially a thrusting weapon. A baselard, also in use at this period was a larger weapon with a larger, wider blade and a simple hilt shaped like a capital I. Civilians as well as soldiers often carried a ballock or kidney dagger which had a hilt fashioned entirely from wood and whose guard was formed by two small lobes projecting from either side of the grip. The simplicity of design and construction ensured a long life for this type of dagger and it was in general use until the 17th

PLATE 8   Hilt of a very fine Dragoon officer's sword,
both blade and guard being finely pierced. The blade
is 17th century whilst the hilt is mid-18th century.
As in many swords the grip is covered with shagreen
and bound with copper wire. Blade 41 inches. English.

century. Popular in Spain was the ear dagger, so called because of its pommel which was formed by two slightly diverging discs, somewhat reminiscent of the pommels on Near Eastern *yataghans*.

Some weapons like the *cinquedea* may be considered as short swords or very long daggers, for their blades vary enormously in length. They derive their name from the Italian words meaning five fingers, which is traditionally the width across the top of the blade. Grips are of the sandwich type with two scales of ivory or bone riveted to a shaped extension of the blade.

As was pointed out above, some schools of fencing emphasised the use of a dagger to parry an opponent's blade and these left-hand daggers were commonly made in a variety of styles. Some are distinguished only by a ring on one side of the quillons whilst a few are fitted with blades serrated on one edge to entangle an opponent's blade. The Spanish *main gauche* with its wide knuckle guards enjoyed only a brief popularity in most of Europe, although it lingered on in Spain until very much later.

During the 17th and early 18th centuries it was common practice for artillery men to carry a dagger which was adapted for use as a measuring and calculating device. Gunner's stilettoes almost invariably had long, stiff, triangular blades and one of the blade faces was engraved with a series of lines and numbers. By measuring the bore or inside diameter of the gun barrel with the blade the gunner could then read off the correct weight of shot required. A variety of scales were used and a few blades will be found with three sets to give readings for lead, iron or stone shot. Grips are frequently of wood, but many are all steel.

Very similar in shape are the common everyday 17th-century daggers, although naturally the blades are of a different style. Quillons are short and the entire dagger is usually plain, although some will be found with the very typical English silver inlay.

It was during the 17th century that another very distinctive weapon was evolving, for the kidney dagger seems to have undergone a localised development in Scotland to produce the Scottish Dirk. The hilt broadened, the lobes became somewhat less pronounced and the wood was decorated all over with typical interlaced Celtic strapwork. Blades were wider and were frequently fashioned from cut-down lengths of sword blades. Early examples of these weapons are extremely rare, but in the early 19th century a Romantic Scottish revival took place, encouraged by the Prince Regent and Sir Walter Scott the novelist, and this accelerated the already present trend towards greater decoration. Elaborate silver-mounted sheaths and Cairngorms, large pieces of quartz, mounted on the pommel of the dirk as well as the accompanying knife and fork, became the order of the day. Another Scottish dagger was the small *skean dhu*, normally carried tucked into the top of the stocking. Both weapons are still part of the full dress of some Highland Regiments.

Another type of weapon known as a dirk is the small, almost ineffective-looking, weapon carried by many naval officers but restricted in 1856 to midshipmen. Most of the earlier dirks had straight double-edged blades around 12 to 14 inches in length. Far more practical was the curved, rather wide-bladed variety. These are very often found with a pommel in the form of a lion's head. Hilts vary considerably, some have knucklebows whilst others are fitted with differing crossguards either curved or flat.

Swords were carried by most naval officers and differed considerably according to the occasion. The Royal Navy, indeed all navies, indulged in considerable ceremony and for these occasions a light, dress small-sword was popular, but for combat a heavy, often curved weapon was preferred and in all cases the officer was free to indulge his own taste. Official regulation patterns appear to have been established around 1801 but it was not until 1825 that full details were recorded. Three types were specified for the various ranks and two years later in 1827 a new pattern was defined and this had the half basket hilt which is still used today. Blades and hilt details have been varied over the years and particulars of these may be found in the appropriate reference books.

For seamen in a boarding party a cutlass of simple rugged construction was normal issue. Cheap and lacking all trimming, these swords were used in conjunction with boarding axes and short boarding pikes.

As the 17th century progressed a number of changes took place in the British way of life—greater use of cutlery, more settled times, a growing military emphasis on firearms—and all these factors tended to make the carrying of daggers unnecessary. Clasp knives were introduced and these served all general needs except in such places as the American colonies where daggers and knives were carried by large numbers of people until well into the present century. Of these edged weapons probably none is better known than the bowie knife although in fact the exact definition of a bowie knife is very much in dispute. It was named after a man who led a colourful and romantic life, full of high adventure, duels and legendary exploits before he finally met his death fighting for a lost cause at the Alamo in Texas in 1836. James Bowie's original knife is usually accepted as being heavy and long bladed with a clipped point and a sharpened false edge. A very short time after Bowie's death all kinds of weapons were being described as bowies, including many that were merely large sheath knives, and this habit has continued to the present.

Cutlers from Sheffield were quick to realise the potential market for such weapons and soon were producing them in bulk. George Wostenholm was the first to appreciate the possibilities and his knives were of good quality and bore his trademark IXL, but this was soon copied by his competitors. With an eye to the U.S. market the cutlers had appropriate patriotic mottos and exhortations etched on the blades, including many that suggest they were made in the United States. The size of these knives varied greatly as did the style of blade and hilt, whilst most had tooled leather sheaths with metal lockets and chapes. Some bowies were manufactured in India, but these are distinguished by guards which are wider and far more elliptical than those on English and American weapons, which are usually straight and fairly narrow. Indian bowies frequently have a spring catch which clips on to the guard locking the knife into the scabbard. American-made bowies are usually far less sophisticated and often have a strip of brass along the back edge.

After the American Civil War of 1861 to 1865, bowie production decreased and fighting knives lost much of their popularity, and it was not until the development of trench warfare during the First World War that knives were again seriously considered as weapons. Raiding parties from both sides found that they were ideal for the types of stealthy combat that they required. Many of these trench knives were crude in the extreme, but others were cleverly designed and carefully made.

Defeated in 1918 Germany suffered a very severe economic recession and few parts suffered more than the steel-producing areas where towns like Solingen had relied so heavily on the production of weapons. Thousands of skilled craftsmen found themselves jobless whilst attempts to exploit other markets met with little real success. Hitler's rise to power with his emphasis on martial glory offered a glimmer of hope for the distressed areas and in 1933 Hitler was offered, and accepted, honorary citizenship of Solingen. He was also presented with a special token in the shape of a sword, but much more important was the suggestion put forward by the Solingen deputation that it would be beneficial to the industry and appropriate to the military spirit of the National Socialist Movement if daggers were worn by the various units. The Fuehrer and his leaders approved of the idea wholeheartedly. A member of the Solingen Trade School was entrusted with the task of designing a suitable weapon and his choice was based, almost exactly, on a Swiss dagger of the mid-15th century. A simple hilt and a severe spear blade made an attractive combination and the design was endorsed by the Nazi leadership. In February 1934 a firm order was placed and soon Hitler's Brown Shirts—Sturm Abteilung or S.A.— and his Schutz Staffel or S.S. were wearing their official daggers. Other organisations were also issued with specially designed daggers and sidearms and even during the Second World War, when materials were scarce, they were still being produced in quantity. Most bear the swastika and eagle together with appropriate insignia and many have patriotic exhortations etched on the blades. Some, like that of the Red Cross, were practical as well as decorative, for it was made with a saw back and a point cut to serve as a screwdriver.

Not only daggers but swords and hangers were reproduced by the Third Reich and indeed they seem to have neglected only pole-arms or staff weapons.

Staff weapons, or pole-arms, were very common amongst armies of all nationalities of all ages ranging from simple thrusting spears to elaborate halberds. Today in vast areas of the world spears still play a very important part in primitive life, whether used for throwing or stabbing. Spearheads range from small leaf shapes to long, almost sword-like blades, whilst those of the early medieval period frequently had two small bars or lugs at the base to prevent too deep a penetration. By the 12th century these lugs had disappeared and the spear then had a plain thickened point. Spears carried by horsemen are usually called lances although there was no contemporary distinction. A hard wood such as ash formed the 14-foot long shaft and the head was small and leaf shaped. Early in the 14th century protection for the hand was afforded by the addition of a circular metal plate, the vamplate. During the 16th and 17th centuries very long spears, up to 20 feet in length, were called pikes and were used to protect the musketeers from the cavalry whilst they reloaded their empty firearms.

Lances had been largely discarded by the late 16th century, but as a result of the success of Napoleon's Polish lancers they were revived and were carried by many cavalry units during the 19th and early 20th centuries.

Apart from spears the majority of staff weapons seem to have evolved from agricultural implements which the peasant would naturally use when serving in the militia. Bills were originally hedging or general purpose axes and these mounted on a long pole made a formidable weapon especially when a hook-like projection was added to one end and a vicious spike on the back edge. Bills remained popular weapons until the 17th century and were

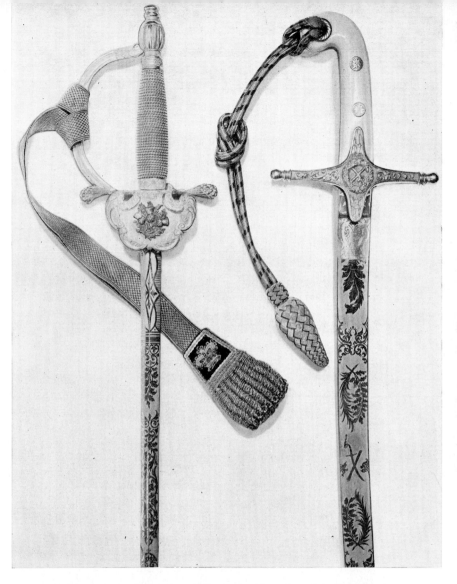

PLATE 9 *Left :* Dress-sword carried by members of the
Royal Company of Archers of Scotland. *Right :* General
officer's sword with ivory grip and decorated blade.
Both these swords were originally owned by the Earl of
Strathmore and are in very fine condition complete
with the original sword knots.

renowned as an English speciality. Similarly the flail normally used for threshing corn was adapted and strengthened so that it could be used to strike a knight from his saddle.

Although most pole-arms became obsolete by the 17th century some lingered on in the form of parade or ceremonial weapons as did the partizan. Originally a fighting weapon it had a long, broad blade tapering to a point and two small parrying blades situated at the base, but ceremonial partizans such as were carried by body-guards were frequently engraved or gilded.

Some pole-arms were indirectly descended from the long-handled axes of the Danes so well used by the English at Hastings. Later weapons like the halberd were in effect simple squarish axe heads with an extra spike at the back and at the end. Originating with the Swiss they were soon adopted by most other European armies and by the end of the 15th century the halberd had assumed its typical shape with a sloping cutting edge, long broad end spike and smaller broader back spike. During the 16th and 17th centuries the cutting edge became more recessed until in its final form the blade assumed a distinct crescent moon shape and the spikes were lengthened. Discarded as a fighting weapon the halberd was carried by officers as a sign of rank until late in the 18th century. Sergeants continued to carry their halberds until 1792 when a spontoon, or broad headed spear, was substituted and these were not discarded until 1830. Spontoons were carried by many continental armies until much later and many bear the cipher of the ruling monarch.

Almost all pole-arms have the head secured to the shaft with long metal arms or langets designed to prevent the head being struck off by a sword cut. During the 17th century it became common practice to cover the shafts with nail-studded velvet and fit around the base of the head a substantial tassel. Both measures were designed to ensure that rain and sweat did not make the shaft so slippery as to prevent a firm hold.

Axes never intended for use were those carried by the guilds of miners in Saxony, for although they have long spikes and broad heads they are slight and quite unsuited to anything more vigorous than being carried in procession. At the other extreme was the pole-axe, for this was a sturdy, almost crude, weapon with a hammer-like head and vicious spikes, and greatly favoured for foot combat in the lists.

This brief survey of edged weapons has, through lack of space, omitted many interesting lines of development and slightly more unusual weapons and it is hoped that readers will find time and opportunity to pursue this fascinating subject further.

PLATE 10   Ghurka *kukri* from Nepal, its shape reminiscent of the ancient Greek *khopesh*. The cutting edge is on the inside of the curve. Traditionally, no warrior will return a *kukri* to its sheath before it has drawn blood. Overall length 17 inches. Blade 13 inches. Nepalese, 20th century.

▶

2

ORIENTAL   WEAPONS

WITH a cheerful disregard for geographical niceties collectors have
tended to lump together as Oriental most weapons originating outside Europe and America. This all-embracing classification is sometimes sub-divided into Japanese and Native or Ethnographical, a
group which usually includes African and similar primitive cultures
—but implicit in this wholesale combination is a somewhat dero-
gatory attitude. Until quite recently there were very few serious
collectors who showed any interest in non-European weapons except
for a number of enthusiasts who accorded a well-merited respect to
Japanese items.

There are several possible explanations for this lack of interest,
some of which are very valid, and probably the most important
is the difficulty of ascribing precise dates and places of origin to so
many of these weapons. In Europe weapon design changed in an
easily recognisable manner over the centuries, but in the East
weapons shown in 17th-century Moghul miniatures differ hardly at
all from those seen in early 20th-century photographs. Certainly
with good quality pieces the style of decoration gives some help as
16th-century patterns tend to be clear, bold yet restrained, and
covering only limited areas, whilst later styles became far more
florid, fussy and extend over more of the weapon. However, at best
this means that a weapon may be ascribed to a century on its
decorative quality, but even this is hardly more than vague. In the

same way it is difficult to say in which part of that enormous area of India, Persia, Iraq or Afghanistan, many of the swords and daggers originated. There was an interchange of styles and cultures all over the East which means that it is extremely difficult to pinpoint one style as indigenous to one specific area.

Whilst accepting both these objections as valid there is still a very fascinating and worthwhile field of collecting and one in which it is still possible to acquire items at prices within the small collector's reach, for the supply is, for the present, still fairly plentiful. For something like two centuries many Britons spent their lives in the East and returned home with bundles of trophies, souvenirs and keepsakes which sooner or later found their way into the antique market. In recent years the supply has been further bolstered because a number of Indian princes have sold off their entire armouries. It may well be that this abundance is partly responsible for the lack of interest in such weapons, but how long this state of affairs will last is very much a matter for conjecture.

The quality of non-European weapons ranges from some very crude stuff from Africa to superb quality swords embellished with enamel and gold from India. There is in comparison with European weapons a larger supply of items from both ends of the scale, and for the collector who is prepared to shed preconceptions and look at the material with an objective eye there is much that appeals. Apart from any artistic appreciation there is a general interest in the specimens as examples of a way of life which is very rapidly disappearing. Even the crudely fashioned primitive dagger deserves appreciation as representing a considerable achievement within the technical limitation of the smith.

Probably most common are the weapons of the sub-continent of India and her neighbours and the variation in style, quality and workmanship is quite remarkable, for they are of every conceivable size, shape and design. Experts assess the value of most of these swords on the quality of the blade, but beginners find it difficult to be quite so detached, tending to place perhaps undue emphasis on the hilt. Old blades were treasured by their owners and often

PLATE 11   A small part of the damascening from the
blade of a Burmese *dha*—a long slightly curved sword.
The surface of the metal was roughened by a series of
scratches—hatching—then silver foil was pressed
down to engage with the rough surface. Width of decorated strip ½ inch. Length of blade 24 inches.

became heirlooms, being rehilted during their working life—thus it is very possible to find 17th-century blades in hilts of the 19th century, or a Persian blade with a Turkish hilt. Good quality blades have a so-called water pattern which is often extremely beautiful, and in addition they may have inset cartouches bearing the maker's name and certain set phrases beloved of the traditional maker. Some blades may bear quotations from the Koran or, far less frequently, some details of the maker and owner of the weapon.

Contrary to popular belief Eastern swords were not always curved and research has shown that the first curved blades did not appear in the East until early in the 14th century. They became more general from the 17th century onwards and as far as collecting is concerned it is a safe generalisation to say that the majority of Indian, Persian and Turkish swords have curved blades. Commonest of these weapons are the Indian *talwars* with their characteristic metal hilt and flat plate-like pommel. The grip usually swells at the centre with two short stubby quillons and there may be a knucklebow springing from one quillon and curving up to the pommel. Delicate silver and gold decoration or chiselled patterns embellish the grip which, in common with the majority of Indian weapons, is usually too small to sit comfortably into an average European hand. Blades vary enormously, ranging from one to four inches in width, either plain or fluted, but invariably curved to a greater or lesser degree. These *talwars* are commonly found complete with their scabbards which are covered with leather or red, green or blue velvet-like material. The mouth of the scabbard is usually recessed to accommodate two long langets which project from the hilt, parallel with the blade.

A sword with a more pronounced curve to the blade is the Persian *shamshir* which has a narrower, but thicker blade than a *talwar*. Some *shamshir* blades will be found mounted in *talwar* hilts, but the usual hilt has simple cross quillons and an inverted L-shaped grip. Some *shamshirs*, especially those of Turkey, have such an acute curve that the scabbard is made with a slit along the upper back edge in order to accommodate the blade.

Easily recognisable is the straight-bladed gauntlet sword—the *patah*—used by horsemen, especially the Mahrattas. A straight, double-edged blade, frequently of European manufacture, is mounted on a steel gauntlet which extends up the arm nearly to the elbow and inside this gauntlet is a single crossbar which forms the grip. Many of these swords are very finely decorated both on the gauntlet and the blade, chiselling and inlay being very common. One version of the *patah* has a very springy thin blade, but this is essentially a ceremonial dancing sword and was not designed for war.

Two very similar weapons are the *khandar* and the *ferangi* and it is only in their straight blades that they differ, the hilts being largely identical. From the thick flat pommel rises a long, slightly curved, spike designed to afford a grip for the left hand so allowing the user to deliver a powerful two-handed swing. *Khandar* blades are usually wider, flaring somewhat towards the point and, almost invariably, have a strengthening rib along the back edge. *Ferangi* blades are either parallel sided or else taper towards the point and are frequently European, for the name means 'foreigner' and the blades are said to be copies of early Portuguese swords.

Indian daggers are legion and differ greatly in detail, but there are perhaps four types that collectors will very soon learn to recognise and of these the easiest to identify is the punch dagger or *katar*. Essentially a weapon of India it is a smaller version of the *patah* and was intended to deliver a punching, thrusting blow. Blades are usually fairly short and triangular in shape, but a few are slightly curved. The hilt is formed by two parallel arms extending rearwards from the blade, and the grip a single or double bar set nearly at the centre of these arms and at right angles. Expanding *katars* have blades which, when the two central bars are compressed, open out to form a three-pronged blade.

Jambiyas were originally of Arab origin but spread over India, as indeed they did all over the Middle East. Their distinguishing feature is an acutely angled blade, usually double edged and often, but not invariably, ribbed. Hilts are the easiest identifiable features

43

PLATE 12 The watering effect produced by the use of
a mixture of iron and steel can be clearly seen on
this *kris* blade from Java.

ranging from those with large fan-shaped pommels from North Africa to the smaller, simpler, flat topped Indo-Persian style. Somewhat similar to the *jambiyas* are the *khanjars* which have a double curved blade and a hilt reminiscent of a pistol butt. Many *khanjars* are fitted with jade grips inset with precious and semi-precious stones. Since jade is such a difficult substance to work and consequently very expensive, it might be expected that such grips were only fitted to good quality blades but surprisingly this is by no means always the case.

Straight-bladed daggers such as the *pesh kabz* are fairly common and may be recognised by the acutely tapering blade which is ground back under the grip to form a distinct step. Another distinguishing feature is the broad T-rib along the back edge of the blade. This last characteristic is commonly found on the Khyber knife which may have a blade ranging from 12 to 30 inches in length, but here the blade tapers gradually from top to point, lacking the characteristic step of the *pesh kabz*. Grips on both types of weapon are of the sandwich type with layers of bone, horn, ivory and even mineral compounds rivetted to an extension of the blade. Both *pesh kabz* and Khyber knives will often be found to seat very deeply into their scabbards leaving only the pommel exposed.

Basically similar in shape to the Khyber knife is the *kard* which is a dagger with a straight tapering blade. Many *kards* have blades whose points are especially thickened for piercing mail—a common body defence in the East. *Kard* hilts are usually very plain and have no crossguard.

Beginners very soon realise that one of the commonest of all weapons is the Ghurka's *kukri* and its lack of popularity is reflected by its low price. Plain government issue *kukris* have little to recommend them, but there are much better quality ones around with fine, silver-embellished sheaths and ornate grips. A complete weapon often has a smaller sheath, affixed to the back of the larger, in which two smaller implements are housed—a blunt sharpening steel and a small skinning knife. An occasional outsize *kukri* may turn up and these are ceremonial and not fighting weapons. Traditionally a Gurkha never sheaths his *kukri* without first drawing blood with it and this custom is still observed by many of these fine warriors from Nepal.

Axes are fairly common and range from ornate tourist pieces to very beautiful and substantial weapons, frequently fashioned in animal shapes and embellished with chiselling and precious metal inlay.

Maces may be similar to the European morning star with a spike-studded ball, whilst another group have the shaft terminating in *khandar*-like grips.

Besides these more common weapons briefly described above there are a large number of more unusual weapons such as the *chakram*, or sharp edged steel quoit of the Sikh, and the fakir's crutch with its metal tipped horn. Far rarer is the *bagh nakh*, or tiger's claw, the secret weapon of the assassin, for this was a metal bar with three, four or five sharp, claw-like hooks and held in place by two rings slipped over the fingers. It could be concealed in the hand until the very last moment when it would inflict a ghastly slashing wound.

Many of these weapons described were not peculiar to India alone and were common in countries such as Persia and Turkey. It is frequently difficult to decide from which of these countries any specimen originates and in many cases the only guide lies in the style of decoration.

To the east of India lies Burma and the commonest weapon from here is the *dha*—a long, plain sword with a gently curving blade, usually in a very plain wooden scabbard.

Further to the south lie Malaya and Indonesia, both areas offering a great variety of weapons. The *kris* is probably the best known and is thought to have originated in Java, probably in the 14th century, but it spread across the islands and each imposed certain characteristics. Blades are either wavy or, contrary to general belief, more commonly straight and have a dull rough, unfinished look to them. It is the hilt and sheath that enables identification although it is not always easy to be dogmatic, but it may be taken as generally correct to ascribe the angular, square-topped sheath and acutely bent grip to Malaya; the oval, almost egg-shaped top to scabbard and grip to Bali; whilst a gracefully upswept, prow-like top and a straight, simpler grip probably came from Java. Larger *kris*-like weapons are known as *kris suluk* or *sundangs* and were used in Borneo and by the Sulus. There are many other interesting and exciting daggers too numerous to include in this summary and it is unfortunate that as a group they have been largely ignored by collectors.

China, despite her great past, did not produce weapons of very high repute and most of those encountered will be of relatively inferior quality although rather eye-catching. Pairs of swords fitting into one scabbard, often elegantly mounted in brass and tortoise-shell, are most common as is the large, rather crude, two handed, so-called executioner's sword with a wide, slightly curved blade, simple round guard of brass or steel, pommel of the same metal, and plain wooden grip.

Japanese weapons are in a very different class and have long been the subject of study and veneration both in Japan and abroad. In Japan the sword was accorded a status far in excess of anything in Europe and each weapon was the result of great skill, reverence and unsurpassed craftsmanship. Members of the warrior class, Samurai, looked upon their swords as objects to be treated with love and respect and handed them on to their heirs as great treasures. This great respect for the sword has meant that many very early blades dating back to the 12th century and before have been preserved and a keen collector can well hope to acquire 15th or 16th century specimens. Swordsmiths were proud of their work and the majority marked their products with their name and date of manufacture. Although the blade was the central unit of the sword almost as much care was lavished on the sheath, guard and other items of sword furniture. Of such quality were these items that some collectors have specialised just in the guards or *tsuba* and many will still be found on the market. The carrying of swords was forbidden by an Edict in 1876 and the craft fell into decay, although never entirely for-gotten, and a few swords are still produced. During the Second

World War a great number of factory-made swords were produced, but it is easy to recognise this type. The subject of Japanese swords is a fascinating and complicated one and those interested will find several reliable and helpful books listed in the bibliography.

African weapons offer tremendous contrasts of style and quality, for in the north the Arabs produced highly decorative pieces whilst the primitive tribes produced essentially practical weapons of crude appearance and manufacture. If anything, African weapons have been even more neglected than others and it is extremely difficult to find any comprehensive source of identification for the number of knives and spears that are offered at very low prices. Most of the easily identifiable specimens originate in the northern part of the continent. Often described as Crusaders' swords are the simple cruciform-hilted swords of the Sudan with blades which had been exported from Germany in the 19th century and clearly marked as such, whilst a few will be found to have earlier European blades. Just as easy to spot are the great sickle-like blades, *shotels*, from Ethiopia and these may occasionally be found in sheaths decorated *en suite* with a shield. The daggers with the large T-shaped grips and the scabbards fitted with a large hoop-like attachment at the back, are the arm daggers of Tuaregs. From the interior come a great number of oddly shaped daggers, short swords and spears and many have never been ascribed to a precise tribal region, although with spears the long blade of the Masai is probably easiest to spot.

This has been a very brief look at some of the more common non-European weapons and collectors will very soon find that there is enormous scope. For general use the book that offers most help is Stone's *Glossary* and recent reprints have reduced the price to such an extent that it is well worth adding to the library of collectors of both Oriental and European weapons. Although some of his information is now out-dated, as it was written in 1934, a great amount is still valid and reliable.

3

TECHNIQUES OF
THE SWORDSMITH

QUITE apart from the difficulty of finding large enough pieces, the very nature of flint precludes its use for long-bladed weapons. Long, thin flakes would shatter on impact whilst pieces large enough to survive a blow would be too heavy and clumsy. A few flint implements large enough perhaps to qualify for the appellation of sword are almost certainly ceremonial or ritualistic objects, but flint was used extensively for knives, lance heads and arrow heads until well into the 19th century. Some cultures used flint to provide an edge for a sword as the Spaniards found when they encountered the Aztecs, for these placed flakes of volcanic obsidian along the edges of a wooden sword. Stone implements which qualify as edged weapons were in use in the Pacific area until very recently and a few collectors explore this interesting, but specialised, byway.

With his discovery of metal, man found that he could now produce weapons with much larger blades than previously, and the early copper and bronze swords and daggers must have been rightly regarded by their owners as infinitely superior weapons. The first impact of sword-wielding warriors upon groups armed only with flint weapons must have been devastating.

Since copper and bronze are both relatively soft metals it was difficult to maintain a sharp edge, but later smiths soon found that iron, being harder, retained an edge for a much longer period. They must also have discovered very soon that iron was not constant in quality, even supplies produced under apparently identical conditions varied considerably. One of the differences that they must soon have appreciated was the variation in hardness, but it is unlikely that they were aware that the controlling factor was the carbon content. High carbon steel is hard, but although this allows a good edge it also means that it is very brittle. Low carbon content means a softer edge but the metal is far more flexible.

An ideal sword or dagger blade really needs two mutually exclusive properties, for it wants extreme hardness to ensure a really sharp edge—quality of high carbon steel—and flexibility with a lack of brittleness—qualities of low carbon steel. The two most common solutions to this problem were to use a compromise steel which offered a reasonable degree of hardness whilst being flexible, or to combine the two steels in such a way as to retain the best qualities of both. The story of sword making has largely been that of attempts to tackle these problems and for the early smith with his poor-quality raw materials, his lack of basic knowledge of metallurgy and his inability precisely to control his furnace, the problem must have seemed almost overwhelming, but in spite of all these handicaps he produced blades of surprisingly high quality. Failures must have been numerous, but when he did succeed in getting just the right combination of heat, metal and forging, to produce a top-quality piece he may well have felt that a touch of magic had come to him. Such a blade would have been treasured by its owner and feared by his enemies, and in this setting it is easier to understand the apparently extravagant praise and claims made about these swords by some of the ancient heroes. Certainly as far back as the 4th century B.C. Etruscan smiths were producing items of outstanding quality.

Etruscan, Greek and Roman smiths welded an edge of hard steel to a core of relatively soft metal, whilst some modern hunting knives are produced by a reversal of this system whereby layers of soft metal are welded to a central plate of hard steel.

Japanese smiths used an extension of the Roman system by putting a hard skin completely around a softer core with the result that their blades were of the finest quality. Many of the greatest

BOWIE KNIFE

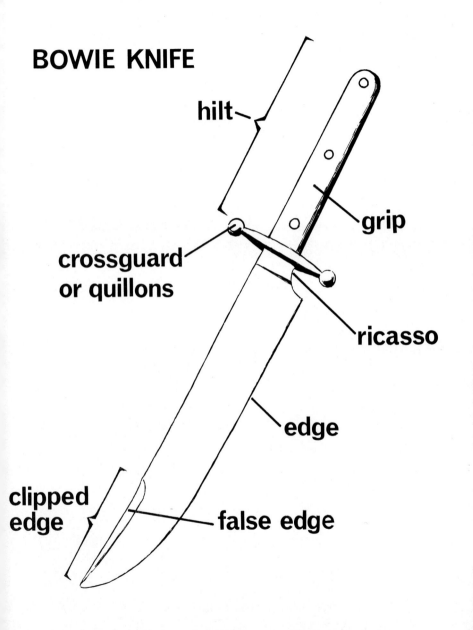

hilt

grip

crossguard
or quillons

ricasso

edge

clipped
edge

false edge

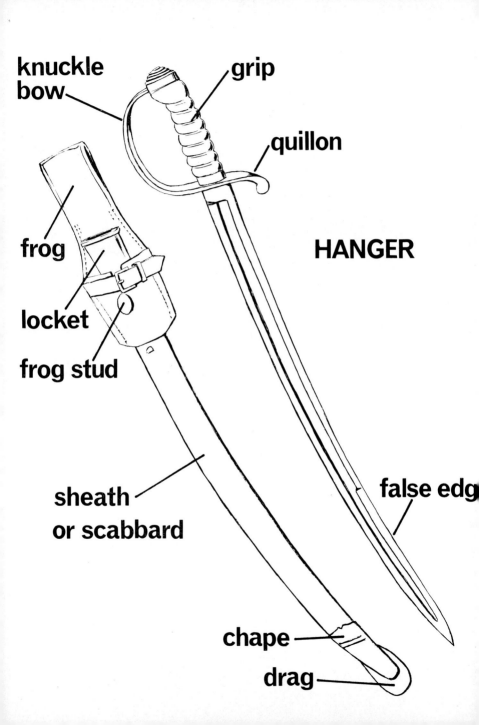

knuckle
bow

grip

quillon

frog

HANGER

locket

frog stud

sheath
or scabbard

false edg

chape

drag

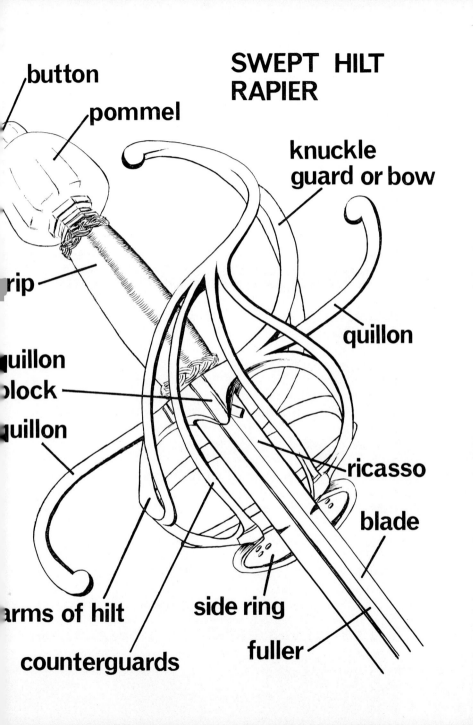

button

pommel

SWEPT HILT
RAPIER

knuckle
guard or bow

rip

quillon

quillon
block

quillon

ricasso

blade

arms of hilt

side ring

counterguards

fuller

masters were credited with the possession of secret formulae and preparations, but basically the process was common to all and the difference lay, not in secret formulae, but in the skill and experience of the smith. The foundation of the blade was a steel plate about five inches by three inches on to which was welded a metal handle. On this "tray" was placed a mixture of coarse iron, clay and powdered charcoal and the entire unit was heated and, when still hot, beaten on an anvil until it cooled. It was then re-heated, beaten again and a groove chiselled along the centre and the sheet of metal was folded over like a sheet of paper and this heating, beating and folding was repeated as many as thirty times. Constant heating and hammering gradually drove out all the impurities and produced a piece of high grade steel suitable for the outer skin. An exactly similar process was used to produce the central core, the only difference being the smaller number of times that it was beaten and folded. Around this soft core was wrapped the harder skin and the entire "sandwich" was now carefully beaten into the required shape. Now came the final and crucial step which allowed a differential rate of cooling to take place, so producing a skin with a graduated hardness. A coating of clay was plastered over the blade and the layer on the cutting edge was either scraped off completely or reduced to a thin film. Blade and clay were now heated to a temperature of around 800° and then withdrawn and plunged into water. Rapid cooling of the exposed edge resulted in great hardness whilst the clay prevented the rest of the blade from cooling as quickly and so produced an outer skin in which the hardness decreased from the cutting edge to the back. The rapidly cooled area of the cutting edge is of slightly different texture and appears as a wavy edged, lighter section known as the *yakiba*. This heating and quenching was, of course, critical, and to ensure a clear eye and alert mind the smith observed certain strict rituals and conventions before undertaking the task.

Blades were now examined for any flaws or imperfections and those found to be perfect were passed to the polisher—all others were destroyed. Using stone of varying hardness the polishers worked for days producing a superb mirror finish which, on many blades, has survived for centuries. Next the blade was passed to the makers of sword furniture who fashioned scabbards of wood, as well as a metal guard, *tsuba*, and a wooden grip bound with thonging beneath which were two little figures known as *menuki*, often of superb quality. Many of the sword mounts, *tsuba* and *menuki* are so attractive in their own right that there are collectors who specialise in these items alone.

Islamic smiths do not seem to have used similar techniques, but relied on steel with a fairly high carbon content and certainly some of their blades tend to be rather brittle. Traditionally the best blades came from Damascus although, in fact, few, if any, weapons were made there after the early 15th century, but blades with certain characteristics were still known as Damascus blades long after this. Basically Damascus blades were understood to be those with a surface patterned by variations in texture and colouring. This pattern, or watering, was produced in a variety of styles ranging from a slightly mottled effect to the celebrated and most highly esteemed "Mohamet's Ladder" with its steps, or bars, crossing the blade— ideally there were 40 to a blade. Like the Japanese, the smiths of Islam were sufficiently proud of their work to mark them with their names and these were usually set in cartouches on the blade. Unfortunately very few of these smiths have been positively identified, but the most famous was Asadullah who worked in Persia early in the 17th century. Unfortunately his signature was copied by lesser craftsmen so that it does not necessarily follow that blades bearing his signature were from his workshop. Many Islamic blades have a small quartered square with an Arabic letter in each section but this is not the maker's name, only a charm to ward off ill luck.

Far more pronounced than watering is the pattern found on *kris* blades, for the effect was here produced by welding together several grades of metal. Originally the metals were in the form of thin rods and produced a hair-like pattern. Later the smiths were able to use a central steel plate on top of which was placed a corrugated strip of softer iron and, to complete the sandwich, another layer of steel.

This sandwich was heated and forged into shape—a lengthy process for the wavy *kris*—and then heated and plunged into a tank of boiling rice-water which affected the iron and steel in differing degrees and further emphasised the difference in textures.

Early metalsmiths in Western Europe were not always as efficient or capable as Eastern craftsmen and their furnaces produced steel of varying quality, often quite poor. Roman accounts speak of Frankish swordsmen having to stop and straighten their soft, iron blades beneath their feet. Greater skill and experience enabled the smith to better the quality and one system known as pattern welding was particularly successful. A long bar of case-hardened steel formed the core and to this was added a layer of softer iron and this wide strip was now cut into thinner lengths which were heated and twisted, cut and then welded together again and worked to form a blade which was then polished. The combination of varying metals, twisting and welding united to form a number of pattern styles. A hard cutting edge was now welded on to the patterned core and swords made in this way were in use for many centuries although by the 9th century they were becoming less popular. By the 10th century advances in smelting and better quality metal rendered the system obsolete and it was discarded. A number of these early swords have been found with a name, presumably that of the smith, inlaid in large rather crude lettering quite unlike the later discreet marking of names in the East.

By the 11th and 12th centuries swords and daggers were being produced in quantities in many of the larger towns of Europe for most smiths were quite capable of the work involved. A finished sword was usually the product of several men's labours, but probably the bladesmith was of most importance. Hiltmakers fixed guards, grips and pommels and the now complete weapon was passed to the sheather or scabbard maker until finally it reached the girdler who fashioned belt and hanger. Cutlers might well make the entire weapon but equally well might buy the parts and employ furbishers to assemble and finish the weapon before they retailed it under their own name or mark.

Techniques of the Swordsmith

Although early swords were essentially local products certain centres, by virtue of geographical position, began to assume a dominant place in the industry. France, Italy and Germany all became main producers and by the 15th century Solingen in Germany had a Guild of Swordsmiths and a Guild of Blade Finishers and Polishers, whilst nearby Passau and Cologne were equally well known. France had centres at Poitou, Bordeaux in the Savoy; Italy had Milan and Brescia, and in Spain Toledo soon gained a reputation which has lasted to the present day. London never became anything like as important although there are records of cutlers there as early as the 12th century and by the 13th century it seems that there were sufficient to inaugurate a united trade group. In 1365 it was decreed that all sword makers were to put their "true marks" on their products. Such marks were recorded on a pewter plate but, unfortunately for collectors, this register has not survived although some later lists of marks are in the possession of the Cutlers' Company of London. Efforts to ensure reasonable standards were made by the Company and inspections were carried out when any goods found to be sub-standard were liable to confiscation.

In 1606 it was ordered that in addition to the cutler's own mark his goods were to be stamped with the dagger of the City of London arms, a practice continued by some until the 19th century. Sheffield had a Cutlers' Company founded in 1624 and members were also using personal marks as early as the mid-16th century. Solingen had a town mark of a running wolf, but like all these early marks it was often counterfeited elsewhere.

Religious, Civil and Dynastic wars of the 17th and 18th centuries created a tremendous demand for edged weapons and vast numbers of blades were exported from the Italian and even more from the German centres to be hilted by the purchasers. Solingen's reputation was so high that craftsmen from the town were eagerly sought to start factories elsewhere. Some came to Hounslow near London, but little is known about the factory which was in operation during the 1630's and 40's, though it must have been reasonably large since one of its principals, Benjamin Stone, was offering the government

57

2,000 blades with a promise of a further 3,000 ready in three months. Birmingham had some blade makers, for it is recorded that one maker alone supplied 15,000 blades during the Civil War.

Small-swords often had three-cornered, or triangular blades and these were imported and were liable to duty charges, so that a company was formed with the idea of producing this type of blade in England. Despite protests from the London Cutlers' Company a Royal Charter was granted to the Hollow Sword Blade Co. in 1691 and craftsmen from Solingen were imported to set up a factory at Shotley Bridge, between Newcastle and Durham. It was not a successful project and by 1724 was offered for sale, but despite its precarious position it did not finally disappear until about 1832.

Small-swords had very elaborate hilts that required the skill of several craftsmen although blade production had become far more mechanised. Encyclopedists of the 18th century have described in detail French methods and there is no reason to assume that those of English smiths differed greatly. A cast steel bar was cut into lengths sufficient for two blades and then fed through water-powered rolling mills until it was correctly shaped. Blades were now ground, heated and tempered in warm oil, after which they were polished on large grinding wheels and given a final shine on wooden wheels. Hilts of chiselled steel, brass and silver all required expert handling and a large variety of files, rasps, scrapers and other tools were used. Matthew Boulton of Birmingham was specialising, during the later part of the 18th century, in producing factory-made hilts which retailed at prices ranging from £2. 12s. 6d. to £10. 10s. each.

Blade making in Britain had fallen off so much that in 1783 the London Cutlers' Company sought government permission to import blades duty free from the Continent and this provoked a Birmingham tool maker, Thomas Gill, to declare that he could produce British blades of equal quality. In 1786 the Honourable East India Company ordered 10,000 blades and each was to be subjected to a bending test. Of the 2,700 English-made blades 1,084 failed the test; of 1,400 German blades only 28 failed, and of Gill's 2,650 only 4 failed. In addition to the bending test Gill had his blades struck flat, as hard as possible, on a block of cast iron and edgeways on a block of wrought iron and it is reported that some cut through the block.

Modern military and dress swords are made in essentially the same way as those of the 18th century, although, of course, a great deal of hand hammering has been replaced by mechanical hammers which shape the blade. Tang and blade are made in one contrary to earlier practice where the tang was welded on to the blade. Roughly shaped blades are now ground on large, water-cooled, sandstone or carborundum wheels before being returned to the forge for reheating and quenching in water or oil. As it is then extremely brittle it is heated yet again and then allowed to cool slowly. A final polish is put on using wooden wheels, leather or even very fine emery.

Decorating has been popular since earliest times and examples of etching, engraving, inlay, blueing and gilding will all be found on blades. Etching was done by covering the blade with paint or wax and into this was scratched the desired pattern or design before the blade was placed in a bath of acid. Unprotected areas of the blade were attacked by the acid which bit into the metal leaving the protected areas slightly raised. Mottos and names were commonly engraved on the blades and damascening was very commonly used on Oriental weapons. The surface was roughened—often by cross hatching—and then gold or silver foil was very carefully pressed into place and rubbed home by a burnisher. A more durable gilding was achieved by making an amalgam, or soft paste, of gold and mercury which was coated on to the blade. Heat was applied and the mercury was expelled, leaving a thin deposit of gold on the metal. This type of gilding was often used in conjunction with blueing, produced by heating the blade to a certain temperature and then quenching it.

Hilts and grips were fashioned from all manner of materials such as gold, silver, copper, crystal, jade, porcelain, wood, staghorn and cut steel. Most common was, of course, the steel guard and pommel with a wooden grip either wire bound or leather covered—perhaps even a combination of the two. Beech and walnut were the two most popular woods.

Techniques of the Swordsmith

In most cases the blade and hilt were united by passing the tang through the hilt and pommel and burring over the projecting tip. Sheaths were almost invariably of wood covered with fabric, parchment or leather, although some all-metal scabbards were used in Britain from the end of the 19th century. A drag, or extra extension, was added to the end of the scabbard around the same period. Belts or supports to hold the sheath were of leather or with some small-swords, a double chain and belt hook.

Sheffield came into its own as a producer of weapons during the 19th century although a Cutlers' Company was founded there early in the 17th century and marks had been used under the control of a Manor Court as early as 1554. It was in the supply of knives and daggers, particularly bowie knives for the American market, that the city excelled. George Wostenholm was one of those who foresaw the probable demand and began producing bowies, marking the blades with IXL. Soon other manufacturers copied this marking and many also added suitable American scenes and mottos. Other manufacturers like Joseph Ridge & Sons and Edward Barnes and Alexander followed his lead and the majority of American bowies were, in fact, British made.

A number of very fine counterfeiters have applied their skill to the production of highly decorative swords, especially rapiers and one in particular, Anton Konrad, executed work that was worthy of the old masters. Fortunately the majority of his products are known since his correspondence was discovered and examined so that it was possible to identify those pieces made or embellished by him.

Modern Sheffield, Solingen, London and Birmingham still produce cutlery and the old skills are maintained—indeed it is already reported that present demands are creating supplies. It is rumoured that copies of Nazi daggers are being produced abroad and it behoves the collector to take care. Germany produces some very fine theatrical swords, but the blades and other details are unlikely to fool any but the rawest collector.

4

COLLECTORS AND COLLECTING

IT is probably more important for the collector of edged weapons to acquire an "eye" and a sense of "rightness" than in almost any other field of arms collecting. Swords and daggers do not, unfortunately, lend themselves to neat, precise, easy classification in the same way as pistols for there are far fewer guides in style, decoration and technical detail than with firearms. Thus it is frequently very difficult to ascribe a precise date or country of origin to many weapons since the same basic style may well have lasted for a long time and have been common to most of Europe at slightly differing periods. Apart from these basic problems the situation is further complicated by the ease with which an over-enthusiastic restorer or an unscrupulous dealer can "marry" blades, hilts and pommels from quite separate weapons. This, of course, is not to say that every sword which exhibits some peculiar feature is a fake for, by their very nature, swords frequently suffered knocks and damage which necessitated some repair or modification. Owners of a good quality blade often had it rehilted in the current style and in an emergency old stock held in reserve might well be used and adapted. Even the marks, maker's names or initials found on so many blades, which might be expected to help, are of little use, for they are so often unidentified or at least unrecorded. Prior to the 18th century our knowledge of makers is very meagre indeed and it is only thanks to the arrival of a more bureaucratic mentality that the surviving trade directories, contracts and letters have enabled researchers to identify many of the sword makers and retailers. The position with Oriental weapons is even more obscure.

Such a formidable list of hazards and confusion might be taken to suggest that this is a field of collecting to be avoided but, in fact, an appreciation of these problems should merely encourage a more careful and critical approach to the subject.

The new collector must first acquire a general knowledge of the changes in style which have taken place over the centuries and with European weapons it is the hilt that gives most guidance. For all practical purposes it may be safely assumed that the general collector cannot hope to acquire weapons pre-dating, at the very earliest, 1500, for these are rare and, invariably, horribly expensive. However, hope need not be entirely abandoned for at least one collector, answering an advert offering a Crusader's sword for sale and expecting the usual Sudanese weapon, was overjoyed to find that it was, in fact, a 12th-century sword in good condition. However, excluding such all too rare events this means that greatest attention should be given to weapons from the 16th century onwards and museum collections, catalogues and reliable books should be studied so that any one style of hilt can be readily associated with its correct period. A word of warning must be offered here for many smaller provincial museums sometimes describe their exhibits with a combination of imagination and *élan* that produces most inaccurate dating, but standards are constantly improving. Contemporary portraits are another very valuable means of identifying fashions in swords and daggers.

Useful as this work may be it is essentially theoretical, and practical knowledge is probably even more important but, alas, far less easy to acquire. It is important to handle as many examples of as many differing weapons as possible but this is easier said than done. How does the beginner go about getting this experience? Fellow collectors are usually most co-operative and contact can often be made through libraries, local societies, museums, national associations and by reference to some of the publications listed in Chapter

8. Conventions and exhibitions, common in the U.S.A., are becoming more frequent in England and certainly offer wonderful opportunities for meeting fellow collectors and discussing the items displayed.

Antique dealers are generally a reasonable and tolerant group but even their patience can wear thin so that it is advisable to ask their permission before picking up any of the stock to look more closely at the details. However, if the dealer does not specialise in weapons it is as well to accept their information about the weapon with a certain amount of caution. Auction rooms afford one of the best opportunities to handle weapons and no chance of visiting the galleries should be missed.

Edged weapons are essentially practical and designed specifically to do a job, thus a sword should feel comfortable and balanced in the hand. If it feels awkward and unsuited for use examine it closely to see if it has been altered in any way. It is to the hilt that one must first look. Any signs of recent filing or alteration to the button may well suggest that the sword has been stripped—possibly only for cleaning, but equally possibly for alteration. Similarly the shoulder of the blade should sit snugly against the rings, or shell, with no gaps or signs of filing. Both hilt and blade should match as far as purpose is concerned and a blade with a *ricasso* does not belong to a hilt with shellguards. Similarly a rapier hilt does not belong to a blade with a cutting edge running the whole way up to the grip. Differences in the degree of rusting will often reveal whether the blade was originally any wider. Grips are of little value in assessing the authenticity of a piece for with many weapons it is not difficult to replace the covering without stripping the hilt and, except on decorative pieces, the grip is probably far less important than hilt or blade.

It is always a little difficult to be dogmatic about blades for they were ground or cut down during their working life. Blades were exported in bulk from several countries, especially Germany, and were then fitted with hilts made elsewhere. Confusion is even more confounded by the practice of some swordsmiths who marked their blades with pseudo-Spanish marks such as "Toledo" or stamped the name of such famous smiths as Andrea Ferrara on their products. Certain marks such as the famous running wolf of Solingen are commonly found and are usually genuine. Many blades bear inscriptions which are either commonplace or commemorative. Commonplace are quotations such as "Do not draw me without reason nor sheath me without honour" and variations on this theme will be found in many languages. Other common themes are cabalistic or magic numbers such as 1414 or 1515 or a series of letters repeated. Commemorative inscriptions are always difficult to evaluate when they claim association with some famous character or event, however, since any such connection will almost inevitably mean a fairly high price is being asked for the weapon, a second opinion is essential. Far more common are swords of the 19th century which bear dedicatory passages, for many volunteer, militia and yeomanry units presented swords to officers upon their promotion or retirement as well as for prizes or other marks of esteem.

Many Eastern blades are covered with long engraved or inlaid inscriptions which are usually commonplace being nothing more than pious passages from the Koran, but on occasions they may supply details of the maker or owner of the weapon. If at all possible it is always well worth having the inscription translated and this can be done by sending a careful rubbing or photograph to one of the national museums or universities with Oriental departments.

A scabbard or sheath can be either a blessing or a curse for it may equally well preserve or ruin a blade. Moisture seeping inside a scabbard can result in very severe pitting indeed and may even weld blade and scabbard with a bond of rust. On the other hand a close fit at the mouth of the sheath can keep out damp and preserve the blade in near mint condition whilst the hilt suffers damage. With all sheathed weapons it is best to withdraw the whole blade for inspection or else serious pitting may be hidden. Leather or parchment sheaths should always be held vertically, point down, for this will reduce strain and avoid the danger of bending or breaking when the sword is withdrawn. When drawing a curved weapon such as the *kukri* from its sheath it is as well to keep the fingers clear of that side of the sheath nearest the sharp edge. Quite often the sheath splits and a nasty cut can be given as the blade is withdrawn.

In the case of a sword lacking its sheath the rusting or pitting— and it is almost certain that there will be some on every weapon— should be fairly even over the whole surface unless there is some very good reason to the contrary. Obviously this generalisation will not apply to brass- or silver-hilted weapons.

If after examination the specimen is felt to be a desirable piece there comes the difficult question of price. Only one rule applies and that is simply that every item is worth just as much as the collector is prepared to pay for it. If he wants it badly enough he will pay the price subject, of course, to his resources. However, unless unlimited finance is available some basis for assessing a reasonable figure is necessary and again experience is the only guide. Auction sale catalogues and price lists are available from the rooms for a few shillings and will give a general idea of the current market value of similar items, but here it is important to realise that no two items are ever identical—condition and detail may well vary considerably. Descriptions in sales catalogues may often be very inadequate, making it extremely difficult to compare, sight unseen, two pieces. Similarly, demand will affect the price and two collectors trying to outbid each other will inflate the final figure beyond the usual level. The location and publicity given to a sale can also affect prices and very similar pieces can realise very dissimilar prices.

With some idea of the current value the collector may then decide how much he is prepared to offer and some consolation may be taken from the fact that, excluding a really bad buy, although the price may be a little high at the time of purchase, good pieces appreciate in value almost daily. If the purchase is being made from a dealer it is usually worth while making an offer lower than the intended price for many dealers will often be glad to make a sale at a slightly reduced profit in order to obtain a little extra working capital, especially if the item has been in stock for some time. Specialist dealers will, of course, have a very good idea of the market value and there is little point in trying to bate this price by very much. With the general antique dealer the position may be more complicated since their lack of knowledge can lead them to over-price ordinary pieces and underprice the more unusual and interesting bits. In all cases the best approach is probably one of subdued hope and not too much expectation.

Persistence is the keynote of successful collecting and the only way to find items is to look for them. No possible source of supply should be overlooked and frequent visits are important even if the initial ones bring no return at all. General antique shops, street markets, auction rooms, jumble sales all are worth trying. Sales of house contents can prove rewarding for sometimes weapons which have lain in attics or decorated walls for many years can provide some very satisfactory buys. As far as the collector is concerned TV, magazines and books have largely enlightened the ignorant non-specialist dealers and the public and the chances of turning up a real "sleeper" or unrecognised treasure are pretty remote. It does happen, but only to the questing collector.

Increased demand for antique weapons has prompted a number of auctioneers to include such sales in their calendars. London alone has at least five firms which hold frequent sales, others are held regularly at Lewes, Birmingham and Slough and there are a number of smaller rooms which have occasional lots of weapons. On the Continent there are sales in many cities of Western Europe, especially Paris and Lucerne, although there is a growing demand in Denmark, Holland and West Germany.

Buying at auctions is by no means as simple as appears at first glance. Catalogues are never deliberately inaccurate but owing to the limitation set by space the description may be insufficient or even misleading. Certain phrases commonly used in descriptions are understood to mean that the piece is of doubtful authenticity or has been modified, and personal examination of the lot and the catalogue description is most useful, for it is then possible to assess the worth of the catalogue. These hazards can make postal bidding a risky venture and there is no substitute for personal examination of the item. If this is not possible then it is very worthwhile considering the services of a commission buyer who will examine the lot and then bid on behalf of the purchaser. His charge is usually a percentage of the price so raising the actual cost, but it does mean that one has not bought sight unseen. Obviously the agent must be given precise instructions as to the top figure, but a reliable one should be allowed a certain latitude since a small extra bid can sometimes make all the difference. If bidding personally it is important to mark the catalogue with the top figure that one is prepared to pay and stick to it. Excitement can make it terribly easy to feel that just one more bid will make the purchase and before one has realised it the price is well above the intended figure. If bids are made outside Britain it must be remembered that in many countries both vendor and purchaser pay the auctioneer, so the final bid does not represent the actual price since an extra percentage must be added to this figure. Similarly certain countries have restrictions on the import or export of antiques and it is essential to check these before undertaking any overseas purchases.

Selling is just as important as buying, since the collector, except for the wealthiest, will have to dispose of pieces in order to raise money for the acquisition of better quality items. Private sales are usually best since there are no commissions or fees to pay but, of course, it is not always easy to find a private buyer at the particular time one wants to sell and this means using the services of a dealer or auctioneer. Some dealers will display items on a sale or return basis and accept a percentage of the price realised as their fee, but more often they prefer a direct purchase from the collector. Their offering price will be based on the value of the item less their anticipated profit and will almost certainly be below the price paid by a private collector. Auction rooms may offer a better outlet but often involve some delay since it is necessary to await an appropriate sale and there is usually a further delay before the final settlement is made. Commission charged varies, but in Britain is usually about 10% and in other countries may be as high as 25%. When handing in the item to be sold a full description should be given as well as the reserve or lowest price at which the lot may be sold. If in doubt the auctioneer can usually advise as to a reasonable figure.

Despite all the advice offered and knowledge gained it is almost inevitable that every collector will make mistakes and buy an occasional doubtful piece, but even this is not an unmitigated loss. Experience is all important and every wrong decision can prove almost as useful as every right one.

5

DISPLAY AND CARE

As each new item is added to the collection there are several things to be done, but most important is the preliminary cleaning. Rust is the collector's prime enemy and it is very rare to find any weapon without some rusting and the first step must be to control any that is present and at the same time reduce the chances of any fresh patches appearing. Patches of hard blackened rust should be removed by scratching them with a copper coin which, being softer than steel, will not mark the surface and the entire weapon should then be wiped over with an oily rag. The oil can be left to soak into any existing rust to facilitate later cleaning and at this time a close examination can be carried out to decide what further cleaning or restoration is required.

Before any polishing is carried out it is always worth scrubbing the entire surface with a strong detergent and stiffish brush for this will remove a surprising amount of ingrained dirt but it is most important to ensure that the specimen is thoroughly dried. It is now easy to assess how much cleaning is required and it should be stressed that it is always better to underclean rather than overclean. Dealers, and not a few collectors pressed for time, often turn at once to the buffing wheel and it must be agreed that this is a quick, convenient method of restoring a pristine brightness to the steel, but it is not to be recommended, for there are inherent dangers. Inscriptions, inlay, marks, blueing and gilding may all be destroyed in the process and it is much better to use a slower, but safer, method. Fine oiled emery cloth, steel wool or, best of all, jeweller's emery, available in a wide range of textures, should be used and worked gradually over the whole surface. Blades present few problems and normally require only care, patience and elbow grease, but to ensure an even finish the jeweller's emery can be fastened to a wooden block, the face of which has been covered with layers of thick material, foam plastic or rubber. The resilience of this pad enables the emery to follow the contours of the blade to ensure an even finish. As the rust is gradually removed a finer grade of paper can be substituted until the finest, scarcely more than rough paper, is used to give a fine, mirror finish. Any inlay must be treated with caution and only the gentlest pressure should be applied to brass, copper and gold and on no account should any abrasive be used on the very typical silver and gold decoration found on the grips of many Indian weapons. Very thin silver or gold foil is gently hammered on to the surface of the metal which has been hatched or roughened and any strong rubbing will remove the entire surface. Soap and water and perhaps a gentle metal polish is the best that can be done in the way of cleaning. Blued metal will not rust, but any scratches which destroy the protective coloured skin will expose the bare metal and rusting will occur. Should this happen there is no remedy but to remove the rust even if it means destroying some of the blueing as well. It is probably not wise to attempt any reblueing as the result is likely to appear worse than the fault.

Plain steel hilts can be treated in exactly the same way as the blades although their very shape makes the job more difficult and time consuming since there are so many awkward corners to reach. Emery can be fastened around sticks to reach inside, but there is no easy short cut. Brass hilts may require a gentle rub with an abrasive if the tarnishing is very bad, although gentler chemical cleaners should always be tried first. Silver hilts will respond well to modern cleaners and the use of long lasting polishes for both silver and brass will reduce the chore of maintaining a good finish.

A number of proprietary rust removers are obtainable which are effective if used with caution. Surfaces must be freed of all grease by cleaning with a strong detergent or carbon tetrachloride and the mixture is then wiped on. Since the solution is acid its effect is to etch the metal and if left on too long it will bite in to produce pitting. However, if the instructions are carefully followed the results should be quite satisfactory although the surface may have a somewhat leaden appearance and will require a final polish to restore a shine. Steel scabbards present no difficulty whilst leather ones will probably require only an application of a good leather dressing. Broken leather scabbards are not easy to repair as an outside patch looks crude and clumsy and it is difficult, but by no means impossible, to secure inside supports but, if it is felt worthwhile, thick card, strips of veneer or even thick foil can be utilised. Some enthusiasts even make their own scabbards and it is a job that requires a certain amount of skill which many may lack. If a sword will not seat properly into a scabbard which is obviously the correct one, never use undue pressure to force it home for the result may well be a scabbard with the chape ripped off. Such a poor fitting may be caused by a lining which has been dislodged or some other obstruction, or, quite possibly, simply shrinkage of the leather, and in each case there is very little that can be done.

Once the new specimen has been cleaned it is important to keep it clean and free of all moisture and every time it has been handled it should be wiped since perspiration can very soon produce spots of rust. A thin film of oil is very effective in preventing rust but dust and fluff tend to stick to it and it can cause staining on walls, and because of this many collectors prefer some other method. Silicone cloths are simple and effective as a wipe leaves a thin protective layer covering the surface; a light rub over with a good quality furniture polish will have a similar effect. Longest lasting protection is offered by coating all metal parts with transparent lacquer, but there is one serious drawback for it may discolour, so producing a dull yellowish effect and this means that it all has to be stripped off and a fresh coat applied. On the whole it is not to be recommended. Whatever system is adopted by the collector it is essential to carry out periodic inspections and cleanings to ensure that undetected spots of rust do not deepen and spread. Items in an excavated condition have invariably reached a stable condition and require no attention other than routine dusting and cleaning.

Recording should be as complete as possible and collectors usually have their own favourite system, but the two most popular are loose-leaf folders or separate cards. The following headings offer a very full description and may be expanded or contracted as required.

Collection Number	S.1.
Type of Weapon	Naval Cutlass
Nationality	British
Date	*c.* 1800
Overall Length	2' 9½″

Hilt

Pommel	None
Grip	Iron with 17 ridges
Knucklebow	Flat circular with slot for sword knot
Quillons or Guard	Flat iron shellguard

Blade

Description	Straight, single edged with fuller at rear
Length	2' 4½″
Width	1½″
Inscription, marks, etc.	None

Sheath

Description	Black leather stitched at back, brass securing hook and chape
Length	2' 5″
Width	2⅕″

Display and Care

General Remarks Overall slight pitting. See Kennard and May, *Naval Swords & Firearms* Plate XIb

Provenance Auction sale (details)

Value — — —

If a sketch or photograph is attached to such an entry a very full description is immediately to hand for reference or insurance purposes. Some people feel it preferable not to give the value in figures and in this case a simple private price code may be used. A word in which each letter occurs only once is chosen and the letters are given a numerical value—thus in GUNPOWDERS if the letters are numbered for 0–9 the price of £15 is now written as UW. The "value" entry will also need fairly frequent revisions for items continue to appreciate.

If it is planned to insure the collection—and this is a prudent measure—a catalogue compiled on the lines suggested above will be extremely useful, making the job of a valuer much simpler. Nearly all insurance companies require some form of valuation by an accepted authority such as an established antique dealer or auctioneer who will normally make a small charge for his services.

Repairs and restorations to edged weapons present difficulties for, although basically simpler in construction than a firearm, any breakages require a fair degree of technical ability and equipment before they can be tackled. Broken guards and quillons must be carefully measured and shaped, using other examples as a guide, and the new piece then has to be welded into place. Once in position they still require a fair amount of shaping and working to make them less than obvious and for this reason it is well worth having the job done by an expert. Old repairs are almost invariably indicated by a thin line of brass produced by the brazing process. Broken blades can be repaired in much the same way although results are often unsatisfactory and most dealers do not bother, merely putting aside the fragments until a suitable replacement blade can be found.

Any major repair or cleaning operation will involve stripping down the sword, but this is not a step to be undertaken lightly. Basically it is a simple matter, but it can so easily result in damage that if it is felt really necessary then care and caution should be the keynote. First examine the button to see how much the tang has been burred over and if there are signs that this is considerable then it will be necessary to file off this overlap. The blade must now be securely gripped between the jaws of a vice which have been adequately covered with lead or soft wood to prevent the blade being marked. Using a punch of hard wood, or brass, the lower end of the pommel—that side nearest the grip—should now be gently tapped, as evenly as possible, all round until it is loose enough to remove. Some easing may be obtained by the use of penetrating oil, if this can be applied without damage, via the grip. If it is not easy to tap directly on the base of the pommel then pressure must be applied via the shells and if this is the case then extra care is required for it is so easy to damage these parts. As the pommel, grip and guard are removed their relative positions should be very carefully noted so that when the job is complete everything may be replaced as exactly as possible. Cleaning or repairs may now be carried out to any metal parts without fear of damage to the rest of the sword.

Whilst the sword is stripped down it may be felt worthwhile to check and perhaps restore the grip. Any leather covering can be treated with leather dressing, but if it is felt desirable to replace the covering then all traces of the original should be removed and the wooden grip cleaned and smoothed. A piece of good quality leather can then be cut to shape and it is important to arrange that the overlap is in the least conspicuous place whilst the two edges are bevelled to ensure a flat union. Soak the leather in water and whilst still wet secure it round the grip and leave it to dry when it may be removed and stuck firmly into position with a good adhesive. Wire binding is probably best replaced with piano or picture brass wire twisted into a double strand, and if the grip is completely wire bound a great deal of practice will probably be necessary to make a first-class job.

When all the work has been completed the tang should be gently hammered to lengthen it slightly so allowing sufficient to burr over the button. Guard, grip, pommel and any other parts must now be replaced in correct sequence and the blade once again placed in the vice. The hilt assembly should now be gently tapped firmly into position using a wooden mallet or block, and when all is securely in place the pommel must be tapped well down. Finally, using a punch, the tang must be burred over the button and any rough edges carefully rounded off with a file. This routine is satisfactory for the great majority of European sword hilts dating prior to 1800, but about this period many swords were made with a button, separate from the pommel, which screwed into place. It is always worth checking all swords of appropriate date to see if this feature is present.

Loose grips or guards can often be cured without stripping the hilt simply by driving thin slivers of wood—even matchsticks—gently, but firmly, into the gaps.

Oriental swords almost invariably use a very different method of securing the hilt for the tang is set into a very effective adhesive compound which makes it extremely difficult to remove the blade. *Kris* hilts use a much less effective compound and are usually fairly easy to remove by gently tapping and twisting to free the grip. *Pesh kabz* and *yataghans* and many others have the type of hilt fashioned like a sandwich where two strips of wood, bone, ivory or mineral are riveted to a shaped extension of the blade. These grips can only be removed by striking out the rivets, but this is unlikely ever to be necessary.

Many Oriental blades require a different technique from that used for European. Persian, Turkish and Indian swords may be found with fine watered blades and unless they are badly pitted these are very worthwhile renovating. Such a blade should be cleaned as suggested above but not given a mirror finish; it is then thoroughly cleansed of grease and gently wiped with some such preparation as Jenolite, whose acid will bring out the watered pattern. If the results are poor the surface can be repolished and another attempt made. Many good *kris* blades have been ruined in the past by enthusiastic

75

collectors who did not realise that a dull, leaden, rough surface, often beautifully patterned, was correct for these weapons and many have been very vigorously worked over to give a shiny finish. The large *sundangs* differ in that they frequently had brightly polished blades.

Japanese swords and daggers form a very special group and require expert attention as well-meaning, but misguided, attempts to restore a polish will invariably ruin the surface. Blades should never be touched with the bare hand as the surface is particularly susceptible to sweat. Experts recommend a minimum of cleaning, using either the traditional powdered lime and tissue or an impregnated wadding. Stripping is a simple process since only one wooden peg secures the grip to the tang and when this is carefully tapped out the whole assembly comes free. If the hilt proves obstinate it should be gripped firmly in the left hand, the blade vertical, and the wrist struck a sharp blow with the cupped right hand and the resulting jerk will usually be sufficient to free the grip.

Ideally all weapons should be displayed behind glass, but this is, of course, a policy of perfection and quite impractical for the majority of collectors. However, it is important that the weapons should be preserved from damp as much as possible and a dry warm room is best. Peg board is a cheap and convenient foundation on which a good display can be arranged with any number of variations. Fittings may be purchased or simply fashioned from thick copper or iron wire and the board may be painted or covered with material such as the new adhesive plastic coverings.

Weapons such as swords can be suspended vertically from brass picture hooks secured to the wall. Horizontal racks are another popular display system and these racks can be free standing or made to hang from a picture rail. The racks can be very simply fashioned from battens into which are set, at a slight angle, short lengths of dowelling, and swords and scabbards can simply be laid on these pegs. Another alternative is a batten secured to the wall and into which is cut a number of appropriately sized recesses. Weapons simply slot into these recesses and they can then be secured by a thin lath or strip of strong material fastened to the front of the batten.

Scabbards present something of a problem and many collectors feel that, with certain exceptions, they are not attractive enough to be displayed with the sword in position. Possibly the ideal solution is to display the naked sword and scabbard side by side, though this may not be practical or desirable, being very much a matter of personal preference. On no account should the scabbard be discarded, for it is rare for any sword, apart from fairly modern, standard mass-produced patterns, to fit properly into any but its own scabbard.

Pole-arms are very difficult to display since their height generally excludes them from any rooms except those with high ceilings. Some collectors and dealers cut the shafts, but it is a practise to be avoided if at all possible. If, however, it must be done it is better to cut at an angle so that a large surface area is available for any future rejoining. Their weight and length makes it important that they be very firmly secured particularly if they are inclined at an angle. Failure to do this may well have fatal results—literally.

It is as well to remember that all edged weapons were designed to cut or slash and it does not pay to mishandle any. All of them, Japanese weapons in particular, can produce some very nasty cuts, so treat them with care and never indulge in horseplay, for serious consequences to collector and specimens can so easily result.

PLATE 16   *Sir Thomas Fairfax, Knight General of the Forces raised by the Parliament*. A print of 1808, but based on an earlier example for the armour is accurate. The hilt of the rapier is a little imaginative but not wildly inaccurate for the Civil War period.

6

BOOKS AND COLLECTIONS

WITH certain exceptions edged weapons have been rather ignored by writers on collecting antiques. There has been a substantial amount of material published dealing with certain types of swords, rare items and pieces of top quality, but the more ordinary specimens have been but poorly treated. Collectors have to search out much of their requirements from sales catalogues, auction catalogues, magazines, learned periodicals and some museum catalogues.

European weapons have naturally received much more attention than those from the Orient, with the exception of Japanese weapons which are comparatively well covered. African weapons are least well served and there is, at the moment, no readily available book dealing exclusively with them.

All the titles listed below have been divided into those in print at the time of writing and those which are out of print or, for other reasons, less easy to obtain. It should, however, be borne in mind that modern printing processes have substantially reduced the costs of reprinting books and there are several American, British and Austrian publishers specialising in this type of reprint so that many previously scarce books may become readily available.

BOOKS DEVOTED ENTIRELY TO EDGED WEAPONS

Readily Available

Aries, C. *Armes Blanches Militaires Françaises*, Reticules 1, 2, 3 (Paris, 1967)

Books and Collections

Atwood, J. *The Dagger & Edged Weapons of Hitler's Germany* (Berlin, 1965)

Aylward, J. D. *The Small Sword in England*. 2nd Edition (London, 1960)

Bosanquet, Capt. H. T. *The Naval Officer's Sword* (H.M.S.O. London, 1955)

Ellis-Davidson, H. R. *The Sword in Anglo-Saxon England* (Oxford, 1962)

Ffoulkes, C. J. *Sword Lance & Bayonet* (Reprint, London, 1967)

Hawley, W. M. *Japanese Sword Smiths* (California, U.S.A., 1966)

Hayward, J. F. *Swords and Daggers* (H.M.S.O. London, 1964)

Knutsen, R. M. *Japanese Polearms* (London, 1963)

Oakeshott, R. E. *Archaeology of Weapons* (London, 1960)

Oakeshott, R. E. *Sword in the Age of Chivalry* (London, 1964)

Peterson, H. L. *American Indian Tomahawks* (U.S.A., 1965)

Robinson, B. W. *The Arts of the Japanese Sword* (London, 1961)

Seitz, H. *Blankwaffen*, Vol. I (Germany, 1965)

Solc, V. *Swords and Daggers of Indonesia* (London, n.d.)

Webster, D. B. *American Socket Bayonets* 1717–1873 (Ottawa, 1964)

Wilkinson Latham, J. *British Military Swords* (London, 1966)

Zeller, R. and Rohmer, E. *Orientalische Sammlung, Henri Moser-Charlottenfels* (Bern, 1955)

Out of Print or Otherwise Difficult to Obtain

Altmayer, J. P. *American Presentation Swords* (Alabama, 1958)

Bottet, M. *De L'Arme Blanche* (1789–1870) (Paris, 1959)

Bruhn Hoffmeyer, A. *Middelalderene Tveaeggede Svaerd* (Copenhagen, 1954)

Burton, R. F. *Book of the Sword* (London, 1884)

Buttin, C. *Catalogue de la Collection d'Armes Anciennes Europeennes et Orientales* (Rumilly, 1933)

Carrington-Peirce, P. *A Handbook of Court and Hunting Swords* 1660–1820 (London, 1937)

Dean, B. *Catalogue of European Court and Hunting Swords* (New York, 1929)

Books and Collections

Dean, B. *Catalogue of European Daggers* (New York, 1929)
Ellehauge, M. *Certain Phases in the Origin and Development of the Glaive* (Copenhagen, 1945)
Ellehauge, M. *The Spear Traced through the Post Roman Development* (Copenhagen, 1948)
Gardner, G. B. *Kris and Other Malay Weapons* (Singapore, 1936)
Giorgetti, G. *Le Armi Bianche* (Milan, 1961)
Hakusui, I.*Nippon-To—The Japanese Sword* (Tokyo, 1948)
Hayes McCoy, G. A. *Sixteenth Century Swords Found in Ireland* (Ireland, 1948)
Holstein, P. *Contribution à L'Etude des Armes Orientales* (Paris, 1931)
Hutton, A. *The Sword and the Centuries* (London, 1901)
Joby, H. and Hogitaro, I. *Sword and Samé* (Reprint, London, 1962)
Peterson, H. L. *American Knives* (New York, 1958)
Peterson, H. L. *The American Sword* 1775–1945 (Pennsylvania, 1954)
Rawson, P. S. *The Indian Sword* (Copenhagen, 1967)
Robinson, B. W. *Primer of Japanese Sword Blades* (London, 1955)
Seitz, H. *Svärdet och Värjen som Armévapen* (Stockholm, 1955)
Yumoto, J. M. *The Samurai Sword* (Tokyo, 1958)

BOOKS CONTAINING SUBSTANTIAL REFERENCES TO EDGED WEAPONS

Readily Available

Blair, C. *European and American Arms* (London, 1962)
Blackmore, H. L. *Arms and Armour* (London and New York, 1965)
Blackmore, H. L. *British Military Firearms* (London, 1961)
Boeheim, W.*Handbuch der Waffenkunde* (Reprint, Austria, 1966)
Hewitt, J. *Ancient Arms and Armour*, 3 vols (Reprint, Austria, 1967)
Hicks, J. E. *French Military Weapons* 1717–1938 (U.S.A., 1964)
Holmes, M. *Arms and Armour in Tudor & Stuart London* (London, Museum, 1957)
Laking, G. F. *Wallace Collection Catalogue of Oriental Arms and Armour* (Reprint, London, 1964)

Books and Collections

Mann, Sir James. *Outline of Arms and Armour in England* (H.M.S.O. London, 1960)

Mann, Sir James. *Wallace Collection Catalogue of European Arms and Armour* (London, 1962)

May, W. E. and Kennard, A. N. *Naval Swords and Firearms* (H.M.S.O. London, 1962)

Møller, Th. *Gamle Danske Militaer Vaben* (Copenhagen, 1963)

Norman, A. V. B. and Pottinger, D. *Warrior to Soldier* 449–1660 (London, 1966)

Norman, V. *Arms and Armour* (London, 1964)

Oakeshott, R. E. *A Knight and His Weapons* (London, 1964)

Reitzenstein, A. F. Von. *Der Waffenschmied* (Munich, 1964)

Robinson, B. W. *Arms and Armour of Old Japan* (H.M.S.O. London, 1951)

Stone, G. C. *A Glossary of Construction, Decoration and Use of Arms and Armour* (Reprinted 1966)

Thimm, C. A. *A Complete Bibliography of Fencing and Duelling* (Reprint, New York, 1967)

Out of Print or Otherwise Difficult to Obtain

Aylward, J. D. *The English Master of Arms* (London, 1956)

Buehn, W. *Warrior's Weapons* (New York, 1962)

Castle, E. *Schools and Masters of Fence* (London, 1910)

Demmin, A. *Guide Des Armateurs d'Armes* (Paris, 1869)

Ffoulkes, C. J. *Arms and Armour* (London, 1945)

Hoff, A. and Schepellern, H. D. and Boesen, G. *Royal Arms at Rosenborg* (Copenhagen, 1956)

Peterson, H. L. *Arms and Armour in Colonial America* (Harrisburg, U.S.A., 1956)

Pollock, W. H. *Fencing* (Badminton Library) (London, 1893)

PERIODICALS DEVOTED TO EDGED WEAPONS

Gladius (Cordoba, Spain)
Journal of To-ken Society (London)

PERIODICALS CONTAINING OCCASIONAL RELEVANT ARTICLES

Great Britain

Apollo (London)
The Connoisseur (London)
Collectors Guide (London)
Country Life (London)
Guns Review (Leeds)
Journal of the Arms and Armour Society (London)
Journal of the Society for Army Historical Research (London)

U.S.A. and Canada

Canadian Journal of Arms Collecting (Mount Royal, Canada)
Gun Digest (annually; Chicago, U.S.A.)
Gun Report (Aledo, U.S.A.)

Denmark

Vaabenhistoriske Aarbøger (Copenhagen)

Germany

Waffen und Kostümkunde (Munich)

Italy

Armi Antiche (Turin)

Sweden

Livrustkammaren (Stockholm)
Svenska Vapenhistoriska Arsskrift (Stockholm)

Switzerland

Armes Anciennes (Geneva)

COLLECTIONS OF EDGED WEAPONS

Many museums exhibit edged weapons but the list below contains only the names of some of those with a substantial number of items. Many other museums may have items of outstanding interest or small selective groups of weapons and many local history societies, regimental museums, stately homes and similar places also contain pieces worthy of inspection. In Britain the Index publications will often help whilst overseas and American museums are listed in the Museum Association Lists.

Great Britain

London	*H.M. Tower of London*
	Wallace Collection
	Victoria and Albert Museum
	National Maritime Museum
Enfield	*Pattern Room* (Special permission required)
Lincoln	*City and County Museum*
Glasgow	*Art Gallery and Museum*
Edinburgh	*Scottish United Services Museum*
	National Museum of Antiquities
	Royal Scottish Museum

Austria

Graz	*Steiermarkisches Landeszeughaus*
Vienna	*Kunsthistorisches Museum*
	Heeresgeschichliches Museum
	Historisches museum der Stadt Wien

Belgium

Brussels	*Musée de la Porte de Hals*
	Musée Royal de L'Armée

Canada

Toronto	*Royal Ordnance Museum*

Books and Collections

Denmark
  Copenhagen   *Tøjhusmuseet*

France
  Paris   *Musée de L'Armée*

Germany, East
  Berlin   *Museum für Deutsche Geschichte*
  Dresden   *Historische Museum*

Germany, West
  Solingen   *Deutsches Klingenmuseum*

Holland
  Leiden   *Het Nederlands Leger-en Wapenmuseum "General Hoefer"*
    Rijksmusem voor Volkenkunde

Italy
  Florence   *Museo Nazionale*
    Museo Stibbert
  Naples   *Museo Filiangieri*
  Naples   *Capodimonte*
  Rome   *Museo Nazionale di Castel S. Angelo*
  Turin   *Armeria Reale*
    Museo Nazionale Storico d'Artiglieria
  Venice   *La Sala d'Armi, Palazzo Ducale*

Norway
  Oslo   *Haermuseet*

Poland
  Cracow   *Museum Narodowe Krakowie*
  Warsaw   *Polish Army Museum*

Books and Collections

Russia

Leningrad   *State Hermitage*
Central Museum of the U.S.S.R. Navy
Museum of the Engineer and Artillery Troops.
Moscow   *Kremlin, Armoury*
State Historical Museum

Spain

Madrid   *Real Armeria*
Institutio de Valencia de Don Juan
Museo del Ejército Español

Sweden

Stockholm   *Kungl. Livrustkammaren*

United States

Illinois:	Chicago	*George F. Harding Museum*
Massachusetts:	Springfield	*Armory Museum*
	Worcester	*John Woodman Higgins Armory*
New York:	New York	*Metropolitan Museum of Art*
	Ticonderoga	*Fort Ticonderoga*
	West Point	*West Point Museum*
Ohio:	Cleveland	*Museum of Art*
Virginia:	Williamsburg	*The Powder Magazine*
Washington D.C.		*Smithsonian Institution*

PART II

*A
Sequence
of
Photographs*

PLATE 17 *Right:* Double-edged slashing sword with large, five-lobed pommel. Originally the hilt was overlaid with silver in much the same way as was done later in the East. On the quillon are the letters H.I. Length 30⅛ ins. Scandanavian 9th or 10th century. *Centre:* Large wheel pommel, slightly down-curving quillons and a blade with a central fuller. Length 33¾ ins. Italian (?), 13th century. *Left:* Typical brazil-nut pommel, straight quillons and wide blade with shallow fuller suggest that this is an early sword. Length 32¾ ins. German. Late 12th century.

EUROPEAN WEAPONS

SOME one hundred and fifty photographs can do little more than indicate the enormous range of European edged weapons and the most that can be done is to offer a personal selection. Since this book is intended, primarily, for the ordinary collector the emphasis is on the usual rather than the unusual, on the average rather than the outstandingly fine and rare item that none but the luckiest, or wealthiest, can hope to acquire.

Identification and dating are so often matters of opinion, albeit well informed, since in so many cases it is impossible to be dogmatic and there is little that gives any direct help. Modern research is constantly amending and altering, often radically, ideas long held to be obvious but even so there is still much which is but little understood.

There is no generally accepted convention observed when describing a sword since some imagine the sword held point uppermost, in the right hand, whilst others specify that the weapon is held horizontally with the blade on the right. At the risk of being thought perverse the captions are based on the convention that the sword is hanging point down in front of the reader. It is a convenient idea since the majority of the photographs are so set out and most museums exhibit their weapons in the same fashion. In all cases the meaning will be apparent from the text.

Measurements have been given whenever possible, but they can be no more than a guide, for it is very rarely that two weapons, even those of the same pattern, correspond exactly. No account has been taken of the curve of a blade and the overall length is measured directly from pommel to point. Similarly blade length is from the bottom of the hilt to the point.

All the photographs are arranged in approximate chronological order.

PLATE 18 The pommel, rather like a fish tail, is of gilt bronze. A maker's mark is set in the blade in copper— a practice which continued until early in the 17th century. Length 34⅜ ins. Flemish (?). Late 13th century.

PLATE 19 *Left to Right:* (1) A stiff-bladed sword with typical wheel pommel. Length 29³⁄₁₆ ins. French (?) Late 14th century. (2) An early *estoc* or thrusting sword with large flattened pommel and narrow blade. Length 29⅜ ins. 14th century. (3) The fig-shaped pommel has a recess which housed a small shield. Wide quillons are decorated by holes pierced at the ends. Length 34⅛ ins. English (?) Circa 1400. (4) A rather unusual wedged-shaped pommel, but otherwise typical sword of the period. Length 31⅛ ins. Late 14th century. (5) A fine sword with a modern grip and a stiff tapering blade. Length 30 ins. French. Late 14th century.

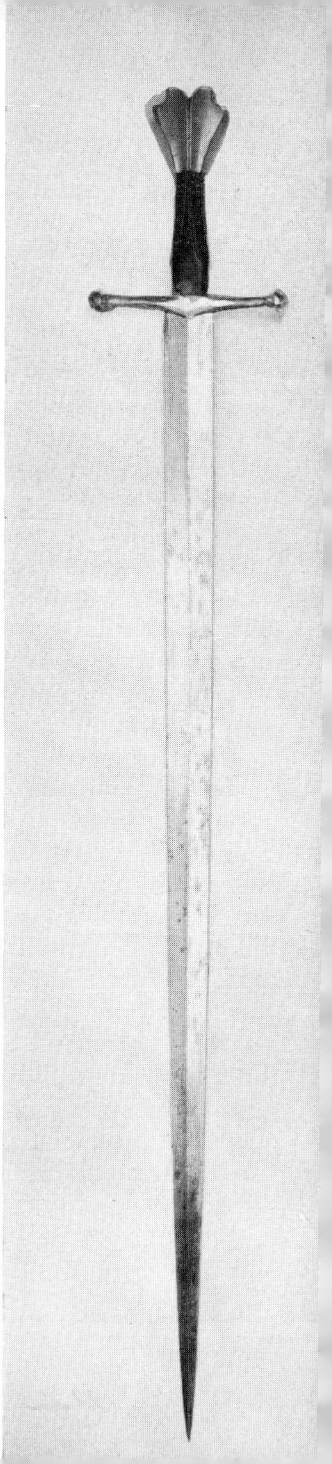

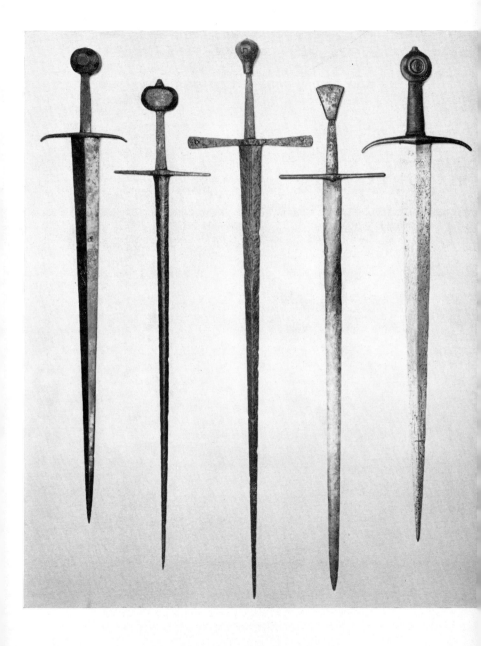

PLATE 20 Pole-axes were formidable weapons but were nevertheless popular during the 15th century for foot combat in the lists. Although that on the left is earlier, the right hand example is perhaps more typical. *Left:* Axe-head length 7½ ins. French or English. Circa 1470. *Right:* Axe-head length 6 ins. French (?). First half 15th century.

PLATE 21 Hilt of a cut-and-thrust sword, the pommel recessed to hold a disc pierced with four hearts. There is a swordsmith's mark on the blade. Overall length $44\frac{1}{4}$ ins. Blade $34\frac{3}{4}$ ins. Late 14th or early 15th century.

PLATE 23 *Left to Right:* (1) Boar sword with the blade terminating in a wavy or flamboyant section just above which a square hole is cut to hold a crossbar. The bar was intended to prevent the point penetrating too far. Length 43$\frac{5}{16}$ ins. German, circa 1530. (2) Early example of boar sword and like previous one the blade is pierced for a crossbar to be inserted. Length 39$\frac{1}{4}$ ins. German. Early 16th century. (3) The early development of the complex guards can be seen on this sword with its blued hilt with arms and counterguards. Length 41$\frac{1}{2}$ ins. German (?) Mid-16th century. (4) *Estoc,* thrusting sword, with stiff hollow-ground triangular blade. Blade length 39$\frac{5}{8}$ ins. German. First half 16th century.

PLATE 22 Hilt of *Landsknecht* sword with the very typical S-shaped quillons. The blade has an inlaid copper mark and the quillons also have simple inlaid copper decoration. This sword is a little unusual in that it retains its original leather covering on the grip. Overall length 36$\frac{1}{10}$ ins. Blade length 31 ins. German or Swiss. Circa 1510.

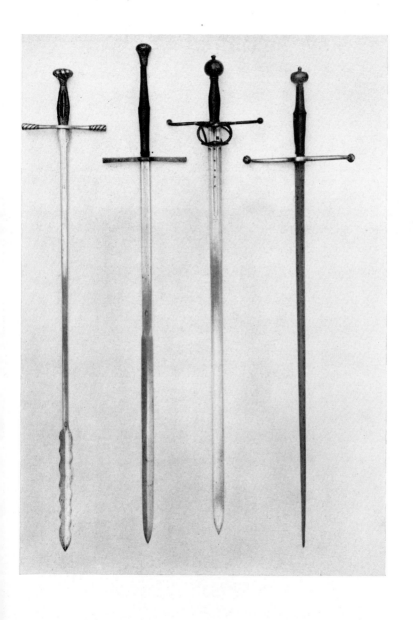

PLATE 24 Hilt of hand-and-half sword the blade
of which bears marks attributed to MELCHIOR
DIEFSTETTER of Munich. Overall length $51\frac{1}{2}$ ins.
Blade $43\frac{1}{4}$ ins. German. Circa 1540.

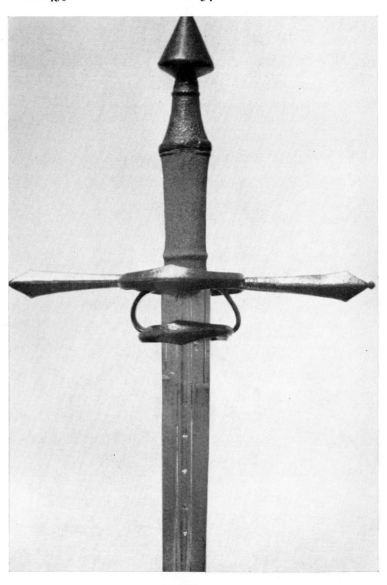

PLATE 25 *Cinquedeas*, popular in Italy, were
so called because they were five fingers wide across
the top of the blade. Essentially civilian weapons
they were often richly decorated with inlay and
often bear etched mottos. *Left:* The ivory grip
is decorated with gilt bronze and the blade is
etched with Classical scenes and mottos. Blade
length 18⅜ ins. Italian. Circa 1470. *Centre:* Very
similar, but rather larger. Blade length 21½ ins.
Italian. Circa 1490. *Right:* Unusual in that
it still has its sheath of black leather on the back
of which is a pocket for small knife and pricker.
Blade length 17$\frac{5}{16}$ ins. Italian. Circa 1500.

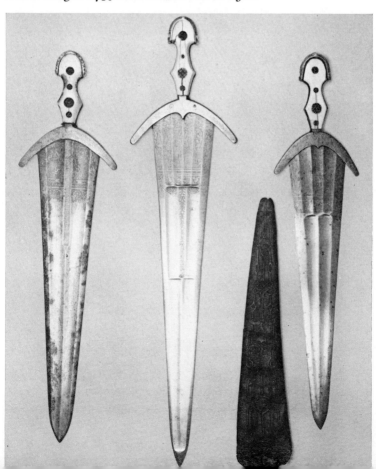

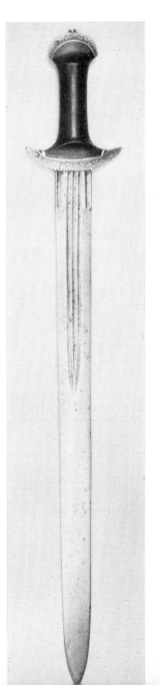

PLATE 26 Another civilian sword called a baselard. The hilt is very similar to the so-called Holbein dagger. Blade length 22⅛ ins. Swiss or German. Circa 1530.

PLATE 27 Selection of 16th-century daggers. *Top left: Rondel* dagger Blade length 15½ ins. French. End o 16th century. *Centre:* Quillon dagger Solid horn hilt with shell guard Blade length 14¹³⁄₁₆ ins. French. Circ 1500. *Right: Rondel* dagger and leather covered wooden sheath. Blade length 10¾ ins. German. Early 16th century *Bottom left:* Ballock dagger and sheath containing small knife and pricker These are also called kidney daggers Blade length 10¼ ins. Flemish (?) Mid 16th century. *Centre:* Ear dagger mad from single piece of steel. The design came originally from the East Blade length 9⅛ ins. 16th century

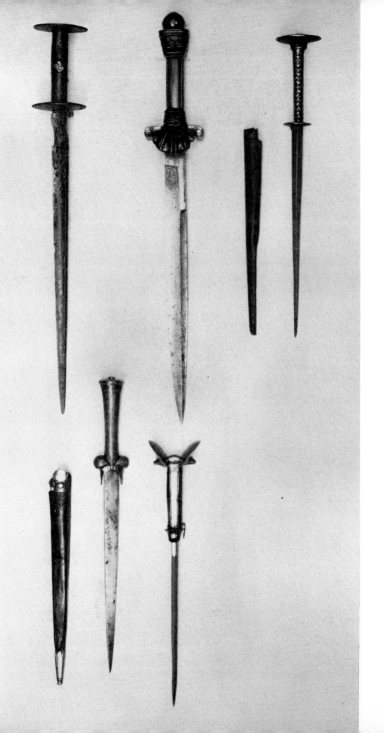

PLATE 28 (a) So called "morning-star" mace with twenty spikes on a round head. Decorated with damascened gold scrollwork. Length of shaft $18\frac{15}{16}$ ins. Milanese. Mid-16th century. (b) War hammer or horseman's pick, a very efficient weapon for piercing plate armour. Hammer and spike $6\frac{1}{8}$ ins. French (?) Mid-15th century. (c) Gothic mace with six flanges decorated with brass inlay. Length of shaft $15\frac{1}{2}$ ins. German. Late 15th century. (d) Another war hammer. Overall length $27\frac{3}{8}$ ins. Italian. Late 15th century. (e) Another mace finely decorated with gold damascening. Length $17\frac{1}{16}$ ins. Milanese. Mid-16th century.

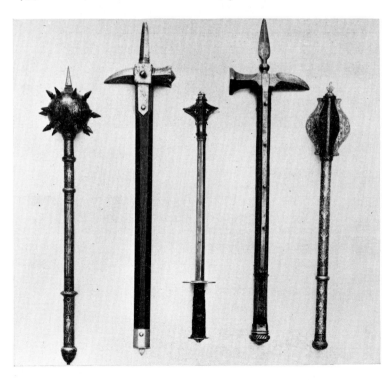

PLATE 29 Hilt of an *estoc* or thrusting sword
with wire bound grip. The long stiff blade is
four sided and is inscribed I.N.R.I. and dated.
Length of blade 36 ins. German. 1546.

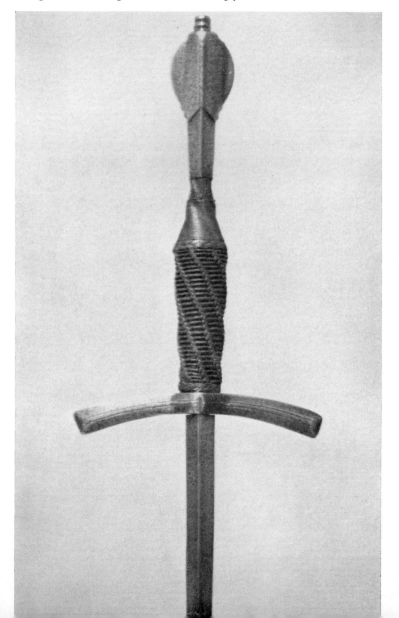

PLATE 30 Large, ovoid pommel and wide spreading quillons—$8\frac{3}{5}$ ins. from tip to tip—make this a fine example of a characteristic hilt of the period. A thumb ring and rudimentary guard form the beginnings of the later, much more elaborate, basket and cup-hilt guards. The stiff, diamond section blade tapers gently to the point. Blade length 37 ins. German. Circa 1550.

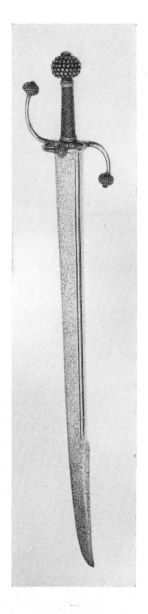

PLATE 31 Pommel, quillon terminals and side ring are all decorated with a deeply chiselled pattern, whilst the straight blade resembles that of a falchion with its 9-in. false edge. Despite deeply pitted blade the weapon is a very fine example of a good quality fighting sword. Overall length 33 ins. Blade $27\frac{5}{8}$ ins. German. Circa 1550.

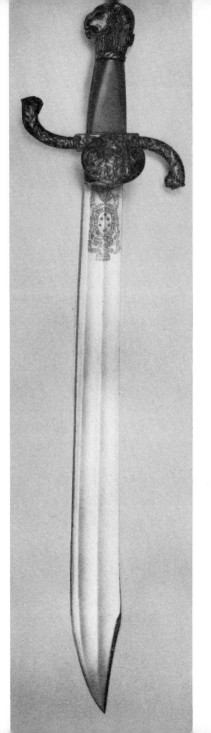

PLATE 32 Very fine falchion-like sword with gilt bronze pommel and modern replacement agate grip. The blade bears the arms of Cosimo de Medici (1519–74). Length 24 ins. Italian. Mid-16th century.

PLATE 33 A Holbein dagger, so called because the sheath has a design based on the artist's *Dance of Death*. It was this style of dagger that provided the inspiration for the first Nazi daggers. The hilt of this particular specimen is suspect. Length $10\frac{5}{8}$ ins. Swiss. Dated 1573.

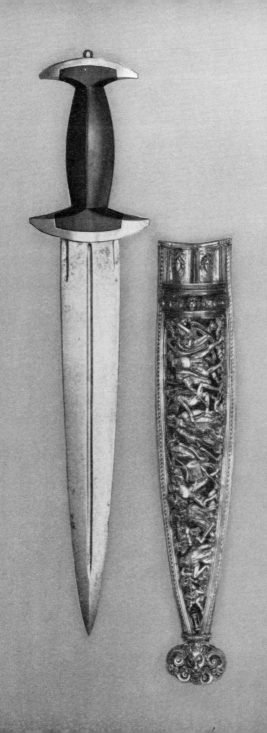

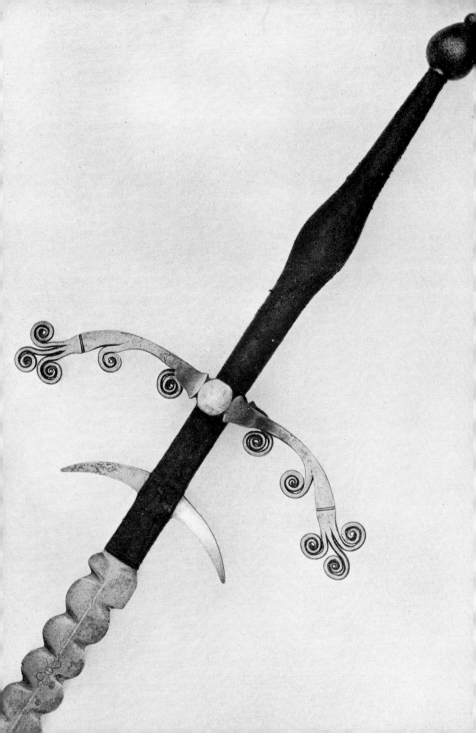

PLATE 34 Two-handed sword with a wavy, or flamboyant, blade which was believed to inflict a more severe cut than a normal straight edge. A maker's mark is inlaid in brass on the blade. The sword weighs 8 lbs. Overall length 5 ft. 9 ins. Blade 4 ft. 2 ins. Swiss or German. Circa 1550.

PLATE 35 Combined axe and wheellock pistol, the barrel of which fires through the head of the axe. The trigger is the button set well back along the shaft. Overall length 40 ins. Axehead 11½ ins. German. Circa 1570.

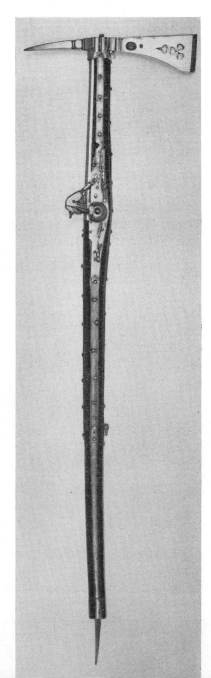

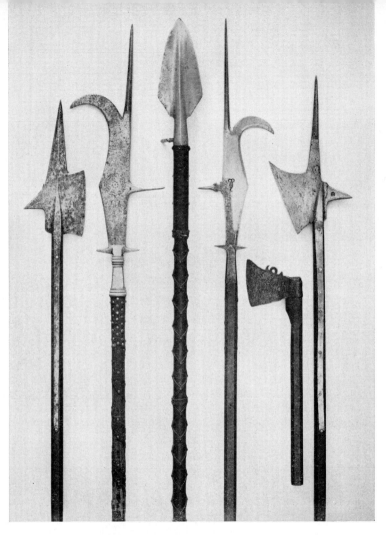

PLATE 36 Pole-arms of 15th and 16th centuries. Left to
Right: *Halberd*—usually known as Sempach type after a
Swiss battle. Swiss. Late 15th or early 16th century.
Bill—Italian. 16th century. *Boar Spear*—a hunting
weapon and often made, like the sword, with a bar across
base of head. *Bill*—bears a rose on blade. Italian
or English. Early 16th century. *Axe*—shaft is
replacement but head is probably German of late 15th or
early 16th century. *Halberd*—a later type with acutely
sloping cutting edge. German or Swiss. Circa 1500.

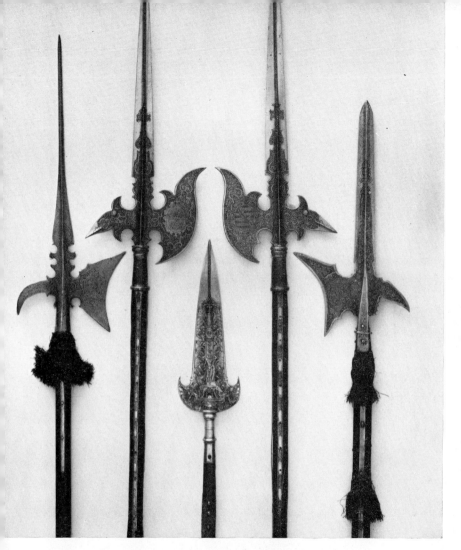

PLATE 37 Ceremonial halberds and a partizan. *Left:* German halberd etched with arms of Saxony and Naumburg. Dated 1610. *Centre:* A partizan of the guard of Henri IV of France. Circa 1670–80. The other three halberds were carried by the Guard of the Elector of Saxony. 16th and 17th century.

PLATE 38 Fine fighting broadsword with large shell
guard, curved knucklebow and heavy faceted pommel.
On the wide blade is the mark of Q. T. crowned and the
inscription ME FECIT SOLINGEN. Overall length 36 ins.
Blade $29\frac{1}{5}$ ins. German. Circa 1600.

PLATE 39 Falchions seem to have been one of the earliest of curved swords in Europe, but the design of the blade varied considerably. Many falchions, like this specimen, have a blade which has a stepped back. The hilt is later than the blade—probably 17th century. Overall length 36 ins. Blade 30 ins. Italian blade of late 16th century.

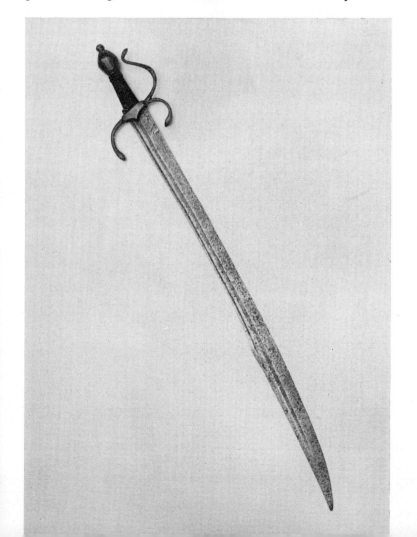

PLATE 40 Swept-hilt rapier with series of plain guards and counterguards. The pierced end to the knucklebow appears commonly on many Spanish rapiers. Overall length 43 ins. Blade $37\frac{1}{2}$ ins. Spanish. Early 17th century.

PLATE 41 Good example of this type of ballock dagger which, although common during 16th and 17th centuries, is now very rare. The stiff, hollow-ground blade is engraved along its whole length and has the remains of inset copper marks. Brass terminals (one missing) cover the ends of the lobes of the all-wooden grip which is probably of ivy or boxwood. Overall length $13\frac{7}{8}$ ins. Blade $10\frac{7}{16}$ ins. English or Scottish. Circa 1600.

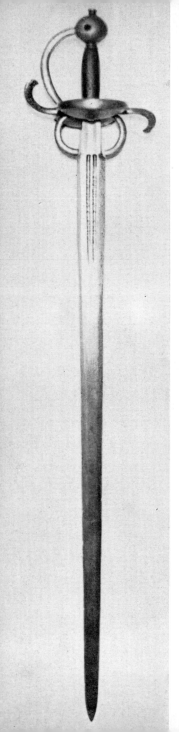
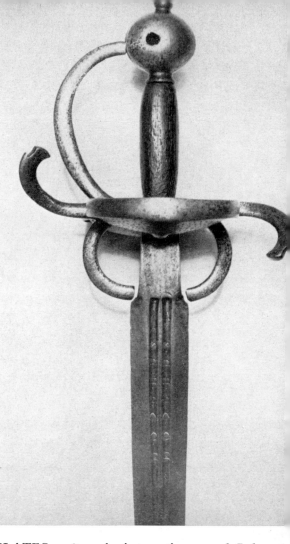

PLATES 42 & 43 An interesting sword. It has several unusual features such as a *ricasso* which cannot be used because there are shells. It may well be an example of an old blade being rehilted. The wide blade has twin fullers stamped with the name of a famous Spanish maker SAHAGOM, which was frequently counterfeited. Blade length 37 ins. English (?) Late 16th century.

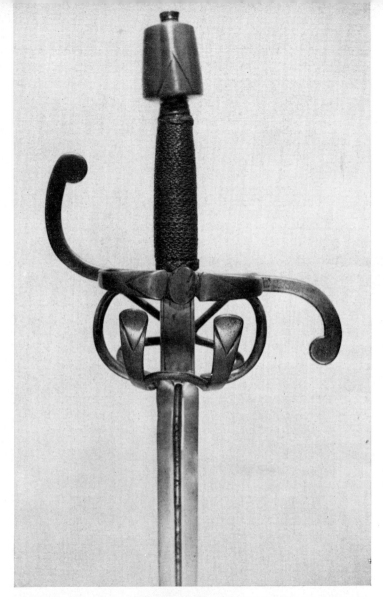

PLATE 44 Rapier with flat quillons and side guards. The blade is of flattened diamond section. Small knuckle-bows are common on the rapiers of this period. Blade length $32\frac{3}{4}$ ins. German (?) Circa 1600.

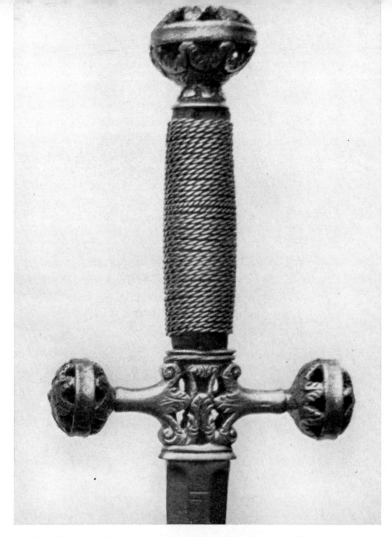

PLATE 46 This type of sword with short quillons and no
shells is known by collectors as a pillow sword since
they were supposed to hang by the bed for self protection.
Blade length 35 ins. Dutch (?) Early 17th century.

PLATE 45 Swept-hilt rapier with large ovoid pommel. Grip
has been rewired. There is an illegible bladesmith's mark
on the *ricasso*. Blade length 40 ins. French (?) Circa 1600.

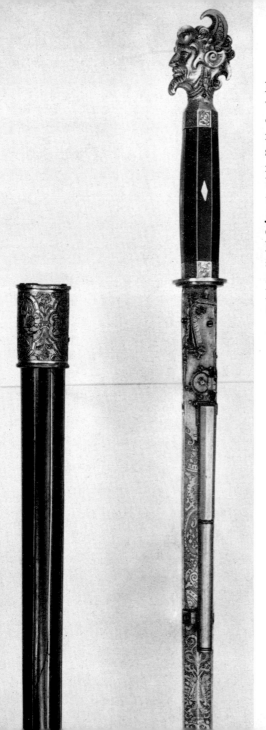

PLATE 47 Rare combination weapon for the long blade is concealed inside a sheath made to look like a walking staff. A wheellock pistol is mounted at the side of the blade which is etched with trophies and the arms of Jerusalem. The fine head is of gilt bronze and forms the handle of the walking staff and the hilt of the sword. Staff overall length $50\frac{1}{8}$ ins. Blade $42\frac{5}{16}$ ins. Barrel $6\frac{5}{8}$ ins. German (?) Circa 1600.

PLATE 48 The double set of down-curving quillons and
large shell have earned this type the name "crab-claw
hilts". This hilt bears traces of silvering. Blade
is of flattened diamond section. Blade length $31\frac{1}{4}$ ins.
Italian (?) Early 17th century.

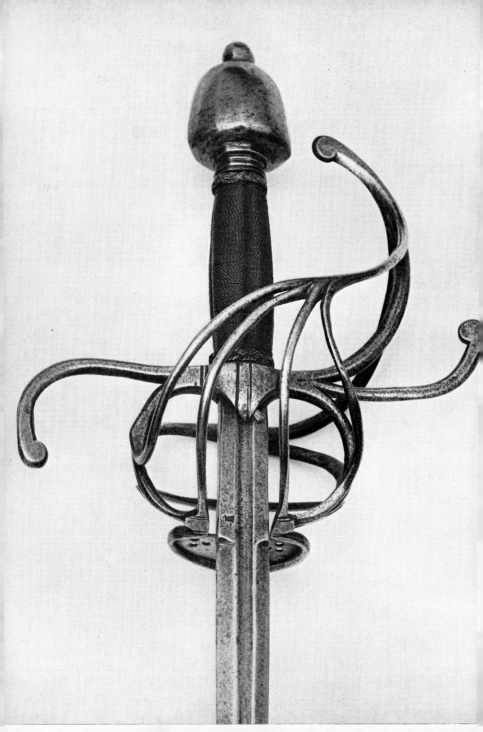

PLATE 50 Rapier with shallow dish with long narrow
quillons. Pommel and dish both decorated with spiral
fluting. Wide blade has single fuller in which is the
running wolf mark of Solingen. Overall length $39\frac{1}{2}$ ins.
Blade $32\frac{7}{10}$ ins. German. Early 17th century.

PLATE 49 Swept-hilt rapier with some of counterguards
replaced by small pierced metal plate. A deep fuller runs
for 10 inches along the blade which also bears traces of
a brass inlaid mark of the running wolf. Overall length
$50\frac{1}{2}$ ins. Blade $43\frac{1}{2}$ ins. German. Early 17th century.

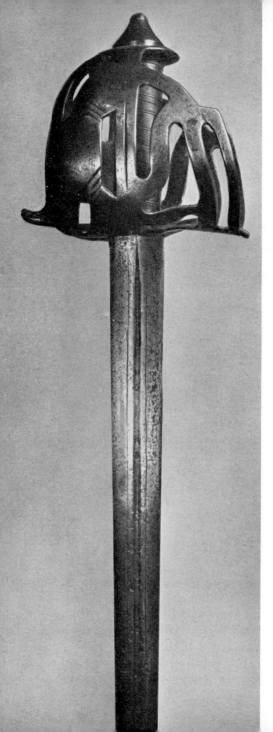

PLATE 51 Scottish basket-hilted broadsword with the hilt exhibiting the projection from which it acquires its name as a beaknose broadsword. Some specimens have painted baskets. A fine example of a rare type. Blade length $35\frac{1}{8}$ ins. Scottish. 17th century.

PLATE 52 Rather unusual style of hilt with the quillons and guards carved with large circular knobs. Punched into the fuller on one side is ANTONIO and on the reverse PICHINIO. Antonio Piccinino was a famous Italian swordsmith whose name was copied by many competitors. Overall length 36 ins. Blade $29\frac{3}{4}$ ins. German (?). Circa 1620.

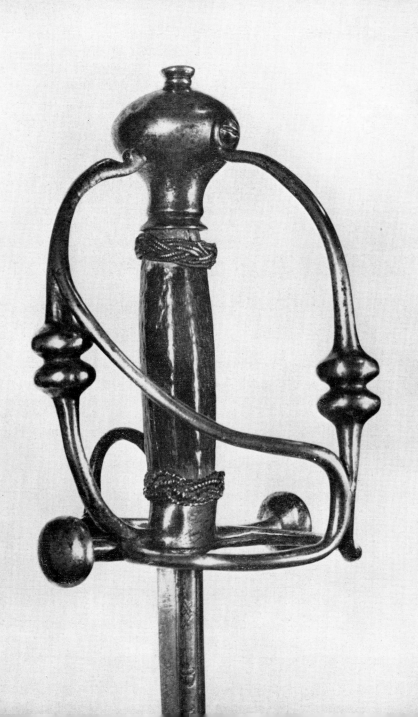

PLATES 53 & 54 Rapier. Originating from Spennithorne Hall, North Yorkshire, this long rapier has a most unusual guard and it is, of course, possible that the repeated S decoration has some connection with its place of origin. The pommel is of a type. There is an armourer's mark on the *ricasso* and the blade is long and stiff with a diamond section. Blade length $43\frac{1}{2}$ ins. English. Circa 1620.

PLATE 55 Small pierced plates have replaced some of the bars and guards—a change that eventually led to the cup-hilt rapier. This type of hilt is called a Pappenheimer after a famous commander. The blade is uncommon for this type of weapon since it is wider than is usual. Blade length $41\frac{1}{4}$ ins. Width of blade $1\frac{3}{4}$ ins. German (?). 1625.

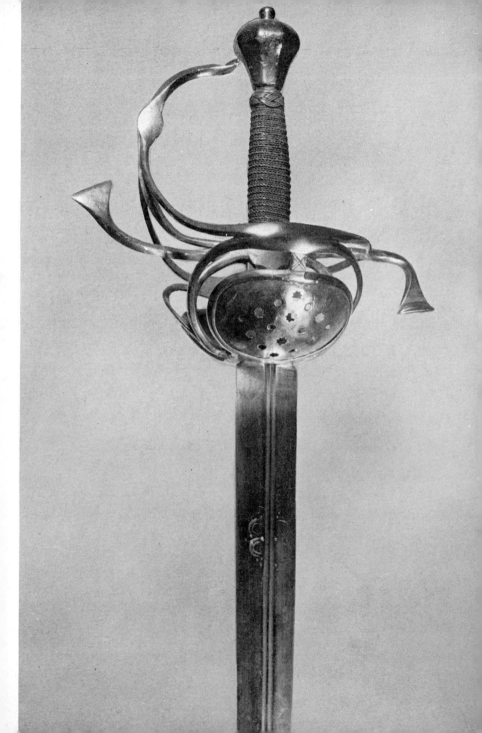

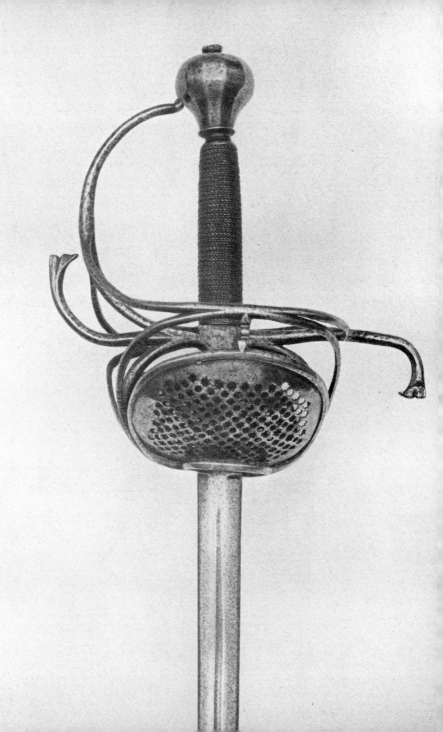

PLATE 57 *Left:* **Blade is probably a cut down rapier blade and earlier than the hilt. Overall length 14$\frac{7}{10}$ ins. Blade 10 ins. English (?) Mid-17th century.** *Centre:* **Left hand dagger with single ring on quillon block. Overall length 15 ins. Blade 10$\frac{1}{10}$ ins. English (?) Circa 1600.** *Right:* **Peasant knife of unusually good quality with ivory grip, silver wire binding and pierced block. There is only one quillon and blade is triangular in section. Blade length 5$\frac{3}{5}$ ins. Spanish (?) 18th cent.**

PLATE 56 A variation of a Pappenheimer hilt for here the shells are larger and pierced with many more smaller diameter holes. The *ricasso* retains its original leather covering. Overall length 49 ins. Blade length 40 ins. German (?). 1640.

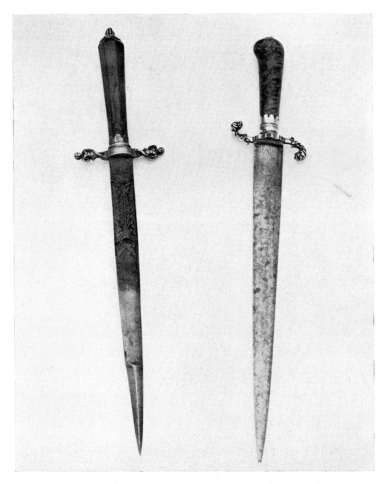

PLATE 58 *Left:* Very fine example of a dagger with
an agate grip and silver quillons. The blade is
multi-sectioned and has an etched and gilt *ricasso*
bearing the initials R.H. Overall length 16$\frac{1}{8}$ ins.
Blade 10$\frac{13}{16}$ ins. Scottish (?) Blade early 17th century.
Hilt late 17th century. *Right:* Burr walnut grip with
silver mounts and quillons and long blade make this
fairly typical of its period. Overall length 15$\frac{7}{8}$ ins.
Blade length 11$\frac{3}{5}$ ins. English. Circa 1680.

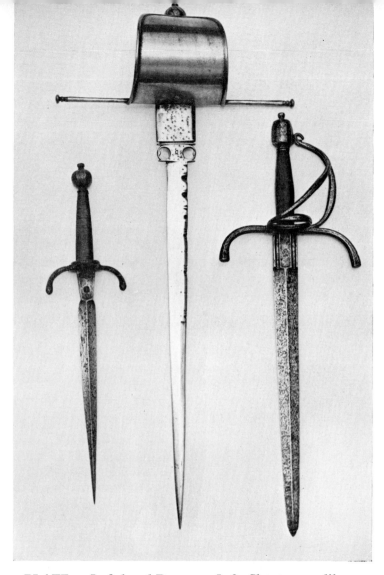

PLATE 59 Left-hand Daggers. *Left:* Short spear-like
blade with *fleur de lys* mark—single ring on quillon
block. Overall length 14½ ins. Blade 9⅘ ins. French (?)
Early 17th century. *Centre:* Typical *main gauche* with
wide knuckleguard and a long narrow blade. Overall
length 22⅖ ins. Blade 18 ins. Spanish. 17th century.
Right: Unusual hilt with knucklebow and guards. Overall
length 17 9/10 ins. Blade 12⅘ ins. English. 17th century.

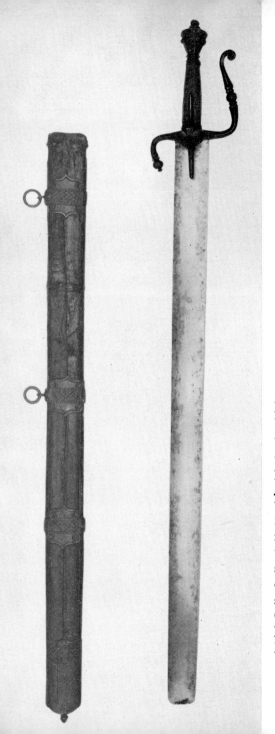

PLATE 60 In Europe
beheading was usually done
with a sword and in many
countries dignitaries were
preceded by a sword of
Justice. Both types had
wide, pointless blades,
frequently with appropriate
mottos etched or engraved
thereon. This is probably
a sword of justice or
ceremonial sword and has
a black leather sheath.
Overall length 41 ins.
Blade 34½ ins. Hungarian (?)
Made about 1620.

PLATE 61 Side view of cup-hilted rapier, the cup
engraved with floral motifs and patterns. Grip bound with
wire over metal strips and pommel spirally fluted. Stiff
blade stamped FRANCISCO. Overall length 45 ins. Blade
38 ins. Quillons 11 ins. across. Spanish. Mid-17th century.

PLATE 62 This view shows typical features of good
quality cup-hilted rapier—long thin quillons, knucklebow and finely pierced steel plate—the *guardo polvo*—
at the base of the cup. Stiff blade is inscribed MONTE
EN TOLEDO—traditionally the home of good quality
blades. Blade length 42½ ins. Spanish. Mid-17th century.

PLATE 63 Common throughout most of Northern Europe, this type of cavalry sword is usually referred to as a Walloon sword. Some have a shell on both sides of hilt, but many, like this, have the shell on the side of the thumb ring missing. The straight blade will be found with a variety of marks—this has a crowned letter P. Overall length $42\frac{1}{4}$ ins. Blade $36\frac{1}{4}$ ins. Dutch. Mid-17th century.

PLATE 64 Hanger or
hunting sword in
style usually
called "Hounslow".
The curved, rolled
end to cap and
shellguards are
typical. Slightly
curved and single
edged the blade
bears the initials
K H beneath a crown.
Length of blade
24½ ins. English.
Made about 1650.

PLATE 65 *Top to bottom:* (1) Short hanger with saw-backed
blade. Steel knucklebow and shell—embossed with man
on horseback. Overall length 22½ ins. Blade 17½ ins.
Late 17th century. (2) Hanger with horn grip, steel
shell and tipped beak—typical of Hounslow made swords.
Blade is stamped on one side ME FECIT HOUNSLOE, on
reverse HENRY RISBY. Overall length 30½ ins. Blade 25¾
ins. English. Circa 1645. (3) Large straight-bladed
hunting sword with very large hilt of steel with horn
grips—single steel shell. Blade has a 12½ ins.
section of saw back. Overall length 34½ ins. Blade 29³⁄₁₀
ins. German. Circa 1630. (4) Hunting sword, horn grip,
steel shell, knucklebow and cap. Very slight curve to
blade. Top of blade has a number of engraved religious
mottos. Overall length 33 ins. Blade 27⅜ ins. English/
German? Mid-17th century. (5) Hanger with curled
"Hounslow" beak to the pommel. Slightly curved blade
with saw back and stamped in fuller—?OLI DEO
GLORIA. Overall length 25¾ ins. Blade 20 ins. English.
Circa 1645.

PLATE 67 Front view of basket of mortuary sword
showing bars with screws securing them to pommel.
This particular specimen has its original sheath
of black leather with steel chape and locket. Blade
length 34 ins. English. Circa 1640.

PLATE 66 Very good example of a nicely engraved mortuary
type hilt. This sword is unusual in that it has a rapier
blade dated 1591 fitted instead of usual, wider, double-
edged type. There is every indication that hilt and blade
have been together for a very long time. Blade length $42\frac{3}{4}$
ins. Blade 16th century. Hilt, English. 17th century.

PLATE 68 Transition
rapier with pommel
and quillon block
both fluted. Two
short curling
quillons and
pierced shell form
guard since this
type had no knuckle-
guard. The blade
is inscribed
ANTONIO PICHINIO.
Blade length 43
ins. In French
style. Circa 1650.

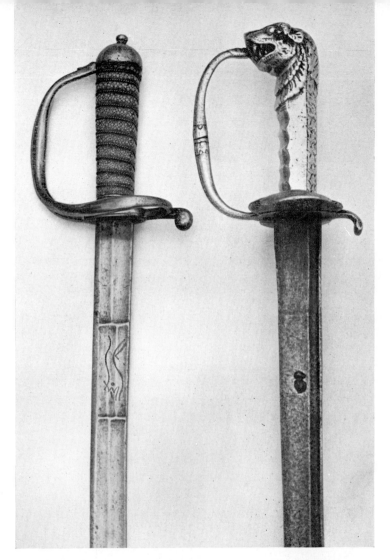

PLATE 69 *Left:* A slightly curved blade of late 16th or early 17th century with running wolf mark of Solingen has here been rehilted as a hanger with brass hilt. The sharkskin grip is bound with wire. Overall length $31\frac{1}{2}$ ins. Blade 26 ins. German blade 17th century. Hilt 18th century. *Right:* Unusual brass hilt apparently showing Oriental influence. The straight single-edged blade bears a stamped mark—a Blackamoor's head. Overall length $30\frac{3}{4}$ ins. Blade $25\frac{1}{2}$ ins. English. Late 17th century.

PLATE 70 Cavalry sword with straight blade signed
SEBASTIAN RUIZ TOLEDO. The grip of fluted bone
is a later replacement. Pierced shells and chiselled
knucklebow with small down-curved rear quillon.
Blade length 32¾ ins. English. Mid-17th century.

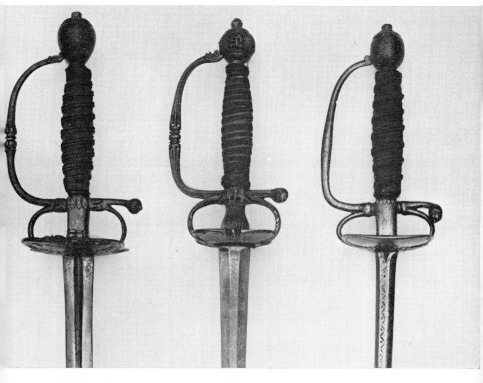

PLATE 71 *Left to Right:* (1) Fine example of early small-sword/rapier with large arms. Overall length 40 ins.
Blade 32¾ ins. English (?) Circa 1650/60. (2) Very good
quality rapier/small-sword with finely chiselled quillon
block, pierced pommel and knucklebow. Wire bound grip.
Top 4 ins. of blade has etched decoration. Overall
length 36½ ins. Blade 29¾ ins. English (?) Circa 1670.
(3) Similar but with very stiff blade and lacking
decoration. Overall length 40 ins. Blade 35 ins.

PLATES 72 & 73 Gunner's *stiletto* fashioned from single piece of steel. Triangular blade engraved with series of numbers ranging from 1 to 120 used for calculating weight of shot. Overall length $13\frac{1}{5}$ ins. Blade length $9\frac{1}{5}$ ins. Italian. Late 17th century.

PLATE 74 By thrusting the hilt of a plug bayonet into
the barrel of an empty musket it was converted into a
short pike. *Right:* Plug bayonet with brass quillons and
usual shaped hilt. Overall length 19⅕ ins. Blade 14$\frac{1}{10}$
ins. English. Late 17th century. *Left:* Although out-
moded by early 18th century, plug bayonets were made
in Spain until very much later. This weapon has blade
inset with panels of mother-of-pearl. Overall length 13½
ins. Blade 9⅕ ins. Spanish. 18th century.

PLATES 75 & 76 Detail of plug bayonet (plate 74) showing brass quillon with crude female figure terminals. The blade is stamped SHOTL-Y BRIDG on opposite sides. English. Late 17th century.

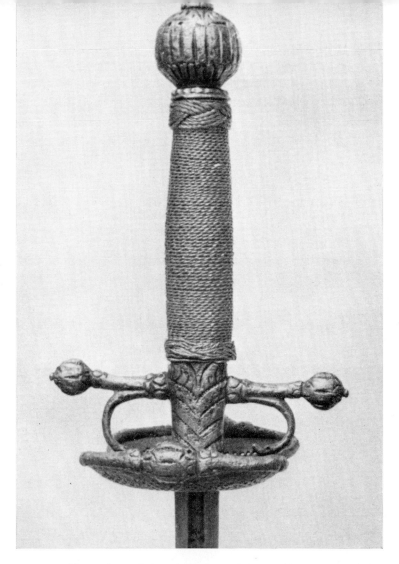

PLATE 77 Transitional rapier with usual short quillons and twin pierced shellguards. The diamond-section blade is signed SABASTIAN HARRANTIZ. Blade length 31 ins. Dutch (?) Made about 1670.

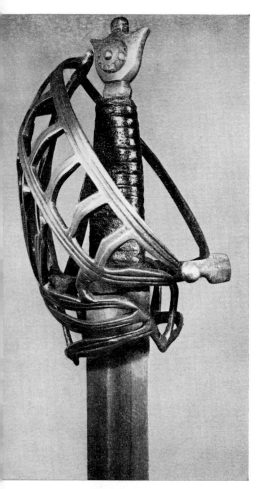
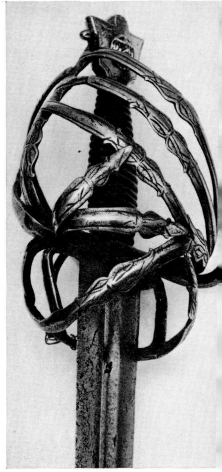

PLATES 78 & 79 Although the *shiavona* hilts conform to
a basic design they vary considerably in detail, thus that
on the *right* has a more elaborately decorated basket and
a brass pommel embossed with a lion's head. On the *left*
is a plainer yet more complex basket and the pommel
merely has an embossed pattern. Both swords have wooden
grips covered with leather. *Left:* Overall length 41 ins.
Blade $35\frac{1}{10}$ ins. *Right:* Blade length $38\frac{1}{4}$ ins. Both
Venetian. Late 17th or early 18th century.

PLATES 80 & 81 A good example of the Scottish
broadsword with a basket hilt pierced with usual
heart and circle pattern, but a little unusual in
that it is further decorated with an inlaid brass
chain and circle pattern. The backguard is stamped
IA above an S. On its blade, interspaced with deeply
marked crowned heads, is ANDREA FARARA.
Blade length 33½ ins. Scottish. Early 18th century.

PLATE 82 Dragoons were troops who rode into battle but
dismounted and fought on foot, and this type of hilt is
usually ascribed to such troops. The pommel is chiselled
into a lion's head and the basket is finely pierced. A
wooden grip was originally wire-bound to afford a better
grip. The blade is slightly curved. Overall length 30½ ins.
Blade 24¾ ins. English. Early 18th century.

PLATE 83 Basket hilt of unusual design with original
wire grip and large thumb ring. The double-edged
blade etched with the Polish coat of arms and
VIVAT AUGUSTUS REX A DOMINUS NOSTER
(Fredrik-Augustus II of Saxony, King of Poland)
and on other side VIN ARC AUT MON ANNO 1708.
Length of blade 32½ ins. Scandinavian (?). 1708.

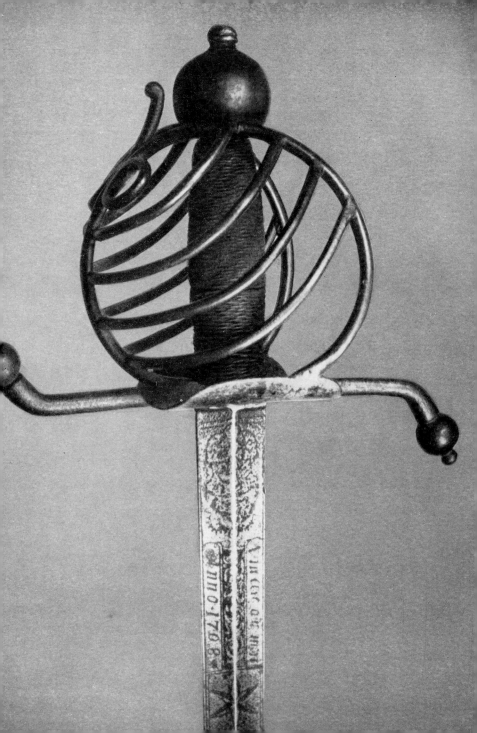

PLATE 84 Silver-hilted small-sword, London hallmark and
date letter for 1724. The grip is bound with silver wire
and the arms of the hilt—usually referred to as *pas d'âne*
in older books—are large and functional. Overall length
37 ins. Length of blade 30½ ins. English. 1724.

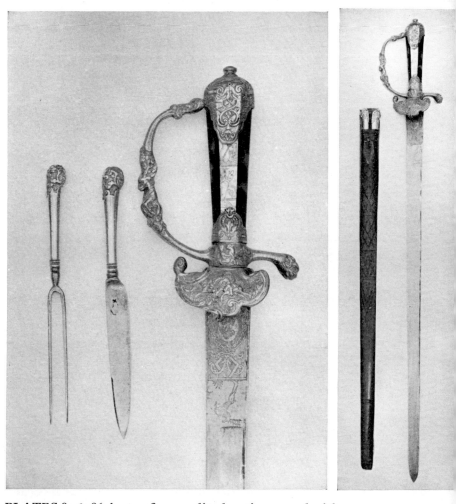

PLATES 85 & 86 A very fine quality hunting sword with
companion knife and two-pronged fork. A small double
pocket situated at the top of the sheath houses the
cutlery and when the sword is seated well in the shell
holds them in place. The top $2\frac{1}{2}$ ins. of the blade is
decorated with etched patterns and a leaping stag.
The grip is hexagonal and decorated with panels of
tortoiseshell and mother-of-pearl. Knuckleguard, pommel
and shell are all of brass. Overall length $27\frac{5}{8}$ ins. Blade
length $22\frac{1}{2}$ ins. Small knife $6\frac{7}{10}$ ins. German. Circa 1735.

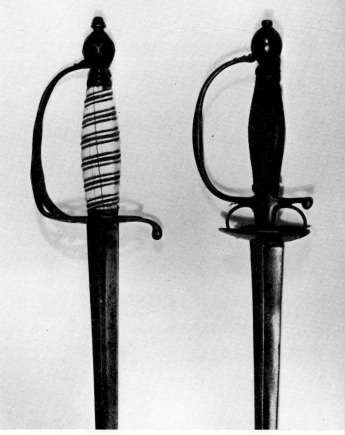

PLATE 88 *Left:* Semi-military sword favoured by officers
as a dress or walking-out sword. It has a facetted
pommel, steel halfguard and ivory grip. The straight
blade is simply engraved. Overall length 38 ins. Blade
length 31⅞ ins. English. Circa 1770. *Right:* Mourning
sword with blackened hilt and a black-bound grip.
Intended to be worn at funerals they were also used,
no doubt, as a discreet town sword for formal occasions.
Hollow ground blade is of good quality, unlike many which
are distinctly inferior. Overall length 34 ins. Length
of blade 27⅞ ins. English. Circa 1740.

PLATE 87 A *trousse de chasse*—a huntsman's set
comprising large knife with gilt bronze hilt and etched
blade and the accompanying cutlery and skinning
implements. The wooden sheath is covered with green
velvet. Length of blade 15¼ ins. German. Circa 1740.

PLATE 89 Officer's sword or Spadroon, a useful, light weapon suitable for decoration or effective use should need arise. An ivory grip is surmounted with a steel pommel of urn form and the straight, back-edge blade bears G.R. and trophy engraved thereon. Overall length $38\frac{1}{2}$ ins. Blade length $31\frac{7}{8}$ ins. English. Circa 1780.

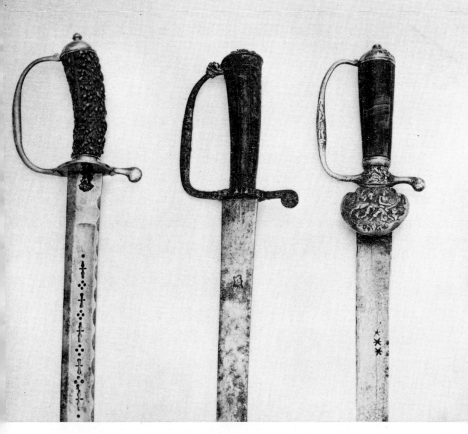

PLATE 90 *Left:* Fine horn grip and silver knucklebow
bearing hallmark and date letter for 1733 shows very
clearly that the equally fine blade has been rehilted
for the blade bears the mark of a Solingen maker working
during the late 16th century. Overall length 26 ins.
Blade length 21⅕ ins. *Centre:* Wooden grip, but the
knucklebow, quillons and pommel of this hunting sword
are gilded and embossed with dogs and deer. Blade bears
a stamped, crowned head. Overall length 24 ins. Blade
length 18¾ ins. English. Mid-18th century. *Right:* Blade
of this hanger is stamped with three stars. Brass hilt
and shell which bears embossed scene of Orpheus with
his lute. Overall length 26 ins. Blade length 20¾ ins.
French/English. Mid-18th century.

PLATES 92 & 93 Brass-hilted military hanger with slightly curving blade stamped with running wolf mark enclosing initials S H—Simon Harvey. On the lower side of the shell is stamped M. CUMBERLAND and 5/38 suggesting that it was a militia weapon since similar weapons often bear county names. This particular specimen lacks the small rear quillon normally found on these hilts. This pattern of hanger is described as 1751 pattern since they are shown in a group of paintings of that date. Overall length 30 ins. Length of blade 24½ ins. English. Circa 1750/60.

PLATE 91 Hilt very similar to that in plate 90 with same type of shell embossed with Orpheus. The grip is of horn and the blade is larger and has deeper fuller at rear edge. Blade length 23 ins. English/French. Mid-18th century.

PLATES 95 & 96 Processional axe carried by miners from Saxony. The blade is purely decorative and the spike terminates in a protective acorn. The shaft is made up of eight bone sections and is decorated overall with engraved figures of workers with the tools of their trade. Length of shaft 23 ins. Axehead $9\frac{7}{10}$ ins. along edge. Dated at back of socket 1752.

PLATE 94 Small-sword of form so often carried by officers. The pommel, rings, quillons are chiselled and the grip is of silver wire. Engraved on the blade are several grotesque faces and blazing suns. Overall length $38\frac{3}{4}$ ins. Blade length $32\frac{1}{2}$ ins. Circa 1750/60.

PLATE 97 Horseman's sword with very fine quality basket engraved with fishes and serpents and wirebound sharkskin grip. Since it is a cavalry weapon the back edge blade is quite long. Blade length $38\frac{3}{4}$ ins. English. Circa 1775.

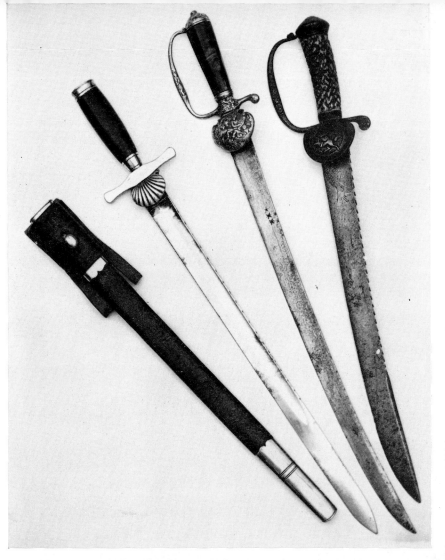

PLATE 98 *Left:* Hunting sword, brass hilt with ebony grip and black leather sheath with brass mountings. Overall length 25 ins. Blade length 19½ ins. German (?) Early 19th century. *Centre:* Brass-hilted hanger with straight blade and hilt typical of its period—here the shell is embossed with Orpheus and his lute. Overall length 26 ins. Blade length 20¾ ins. English. Mid-18th century. *Right:* Early example of hanger (see plate 65 (1)). Sawback edge. Blade very slightly curved.

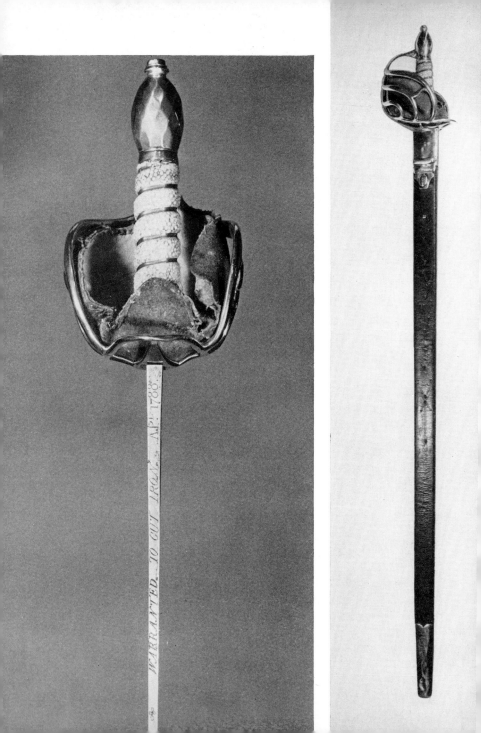

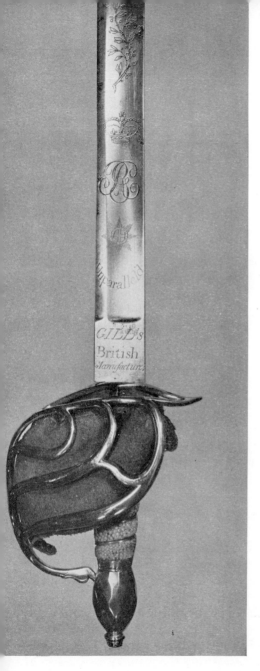

PLATES 99, 100, 101
A very fine
example of a heavy
cavalry sword.
This specimen
retains original
buff leather lining
inside basket-
guard, and brass-
mounted leather
scabbard. The guard
is brass but the
large faceted
pommel is of steel.
A very long single-
edged blade
proclaims the
virtue of the sword
and its maker
(Thomas) Gill of
Birmingham. Length
of blade 39 ins.
English. April 1788.

PLATE 102 Basket hilt of Scottish broadsword usually known as a Claymore. The blade is inscribed J. J. RUNKEL SOLINGEN although in fact this particular maker worked in London and merely purchased his blades abroad. Length of blade 33⅛ ins. English. Circa 1800.

PLATE 103 Hunting sword with bone grip and brass quillons and pommel, the shellguard, not visible, is very much smaller than in most hunting swords. The straight double-edged blade bears the running wolf mark of Solingen. Length of blade 23½ ins. English/German. Circa 1780.

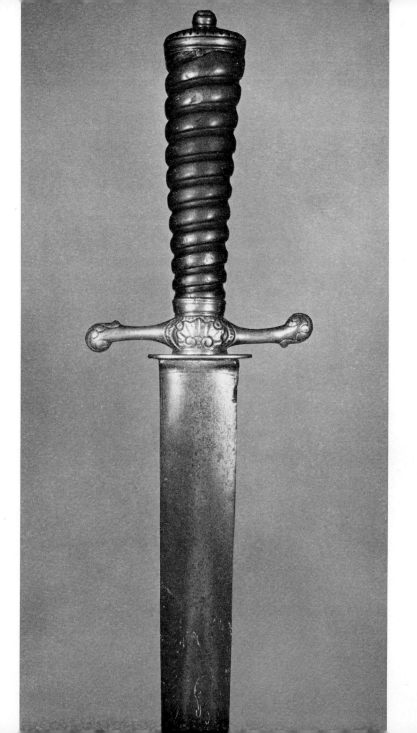

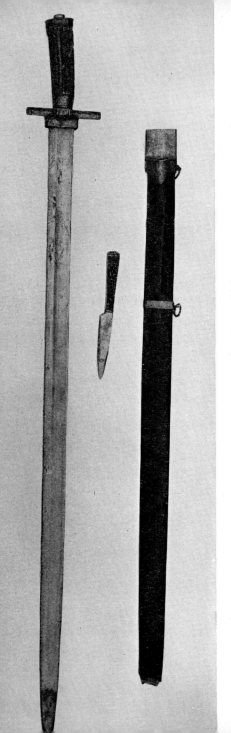

PLATE 104 One of the longest hunting swords encountered. The blade is engraved with the double-headed eagle of Austria. A small shell covers the hilt of the small knife when it is in the small pocket at the top of the sheath. Unfortunately the steel chape is missing from the black leather sheath. Overall length 39 ins. Blade 33 ins. Austrian.

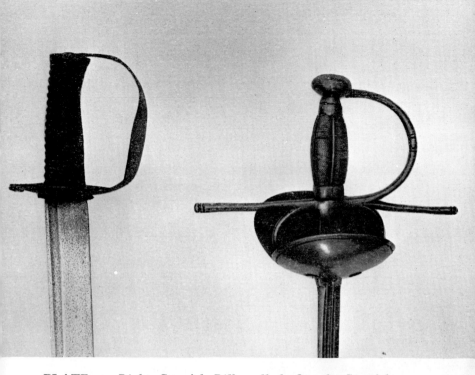

PLATE 105 *Right:* Spanish *Bilbo* called after the Spanish town of Bilbao. This type of cup hilt with its differing size solid shells, copper wire-bound grip, was made until the 19th century. Overall length 41½ ins. Length of blade 34⅜ ins. Spanish. Circa 1800 (?) *Left:* Iron hilt of Naval cutlass of early 19th century. Simple almost to the point of crudity, the hilt is of cast iron and the guard is composed of two discs. Some are marked G.R., some bear makers names, others, like this, have no marks. Overall length 33½ ins. Blade length 28½ ins. English. Circa 1805.

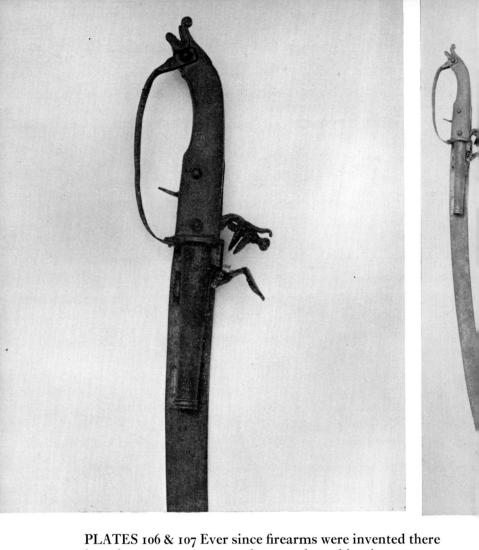

PLATES 106 & 107 Ever since firearms were invented there
have been attempts to produce good combination weapons
and the pistol-sword is the commonest. This has every
indication of being genuine but is the most peculiar
mixture and seems to have been made locally. The grip is
of brass and the pistol lock is crudely made but quite
functional, whilst the knucklebow appears to have been
added as an afterthought. On the sheath was an old label
saying that the weapon was found in Venice. Overall
length 25$\frac{3}{8}$ ins. Length of blade 19$\frac{3}{8}$ ins. Pistol
barrel 4$\frac{1}{5}$ ins. Italian (?) 18th century (?)

PLATES 108, 109 & 110 Fine pistol-sword with straight,
back-edge blade, engraved just below pistol D. RITSON in
script. Horn grip has fluted steel pommel cap, steel knucklebow and shell pierced by two holes. The pistol barrel
bears a ⓥ—Birmingham view mark—and unscrews for
loading. Overall length 30 ins. Blade 24$\frac{7}{8}$ ins. Pistol
barrel 4 ins. Bore $\frac{1}{2}$ in. English. Mid-18th century.

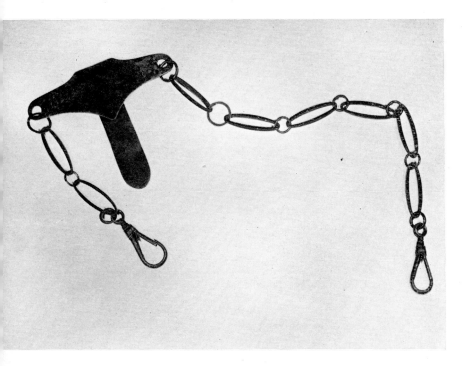

PLATE 111 Small-sword hanger of steel. The two chains, one 11 ins. and the other 5 ins., are fitted with two spring catches and these clipped on to the rings on the scabbard and the long hook slipped over a waist band or belt. English or French. Late 18th or early 19th century.

PLATE 112 Silver hilt of small-sword. Small, purely decorative arms of the hilt indicate that it is a late example of this kind of weapon. Pommel, shell and quillon block are pierced and both quillons are chiselled. Unfortunately the blade, a *colichemarde* type, is very badly pitted and an inscription thereon is largely illegible except for PONT ST. MICHEL A PARIS. Overall length 36¼ ins. Blade 29½ ins. French. Circa 1760 (?)

PLATES 113, 114 & 115 Although a regulation sword,
specimens of the 1796 pattern Light Cavalry sabre will be
found to vary in details since they were supplied by a number
of different manufacturers. *Left:* Light well-made weapon
by JOHN GILL, the son of the famous Thomas. The finish
and general quality is very good. *Centre:* Same pattern

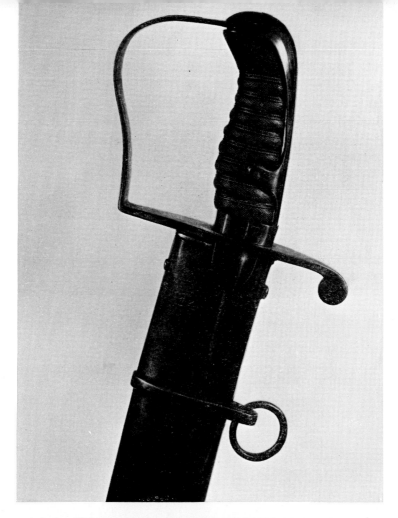

made by WOOLLEY & CO. BIRM(INGHA)M but the sword and sheath are both heavier and clumsier than that by Gill. *Right:* Blade is blued and gilt and the scabbard bears the stamp of 14 LD—14th Light Dragoons—again this is better quality than the previous two. Overall lengths 37¼ ins. Blade lengths 34 ins. English. 1796.

PLATES 116 & 117 *(left)* Infantry Officer's sword of 1803 pattern, the locket of sheath inscribed PITTER & FOX, BEDFORD STREET, COVENT GARDEN, LONDON. The blued and gilt curved blade is engraved with Royal Arms, G.R., patterns and WARRANTED. Brass hilt is of the style used by Officers of the Flank Companies. Overall length 35 ins. Blade 29⅜ ins. English. Circa 1810.

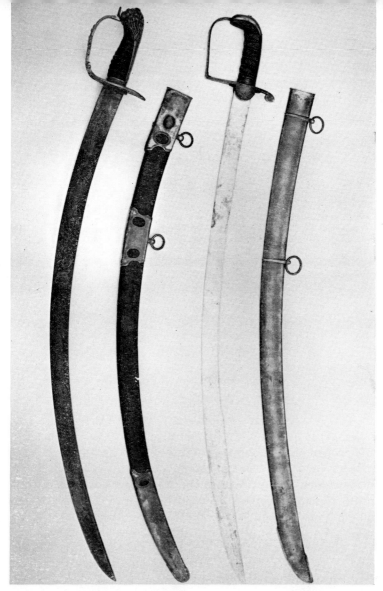

PLATE 117 *(right)* A variation on the 1796
pattern Light Cavalry sword. Almost every feature is
slightly different—the grip has a larger than usual
"nose" and is not unlike that found on Pioneer hanger of
1831; the blade has a very distinct step on the back and
the drag is very small and pointed, unlike the great
majority which are round. Overall length $35\frac{3}{4}$ ins. Blade
$31\frac{1}{4}$ ins. English (?). Circa 1800 (?).

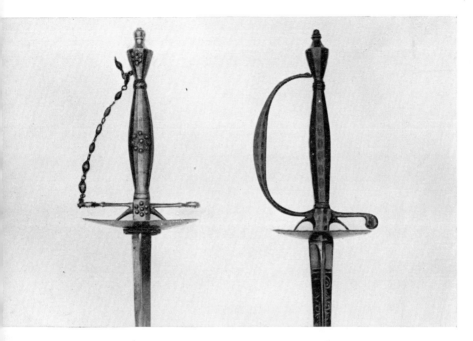

PLATE 118 *Left:* Steel-hilted small-sword with typical small arms on hilt and flat oval disc which had replaced the earlier style of shaped shells. A steel chain has here replaced the true knuckleguard. Hilt and disc are decorated with a number of cut steel studs each separately fitted. Blade marked DRURY 32 STRAND LONDON. Overall length 39 ins. Blade 32 ins. *Right:* The entire hilt is blued and the first 9½ ins. of the blade are blued and gilt. On the locket of the scabbard is LANGFORD NO. 50 FLEET STREET. Overall length 39½ ins. Blade 32⅜ ins. English. From about 1780 to 1797.

PLATE 119 The dress or walking-out sword of Heavy Cavalry Officers, pattern 1796-1834. The back edge blade is engraved with G.R. and several military motifs. On the back edge of blade is engraved J. J. RUNKEL (See plate 102). Overall length 39 ins. Blade 32¼ ins. English. Circa 1800.

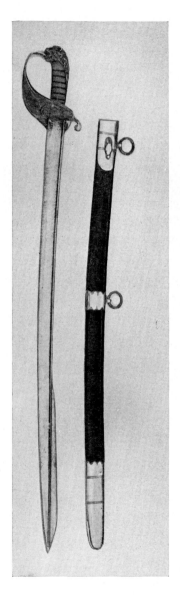

PLATE 120 Naval fighting sword of 1827 pattern with pipeback blade (i.e. strengthening ridge running along back of blade) which widens towards point. Basket has a folding shell which does not, like so many, engage with a stud on the sheath locket to hold the sword in place. Many naval swords have blades etched with patterns and the name of a supplier or maker, but this one has been so overcleaned that all traces of such details have been removed. Overall length 36⅝ ins. Blade 31¼ ins. English. Circa 1830.

PLATE 121 *Left to right:* (1) Ivory-hilted dirk with terminal ball and gilt pommel cap. Bunches of grapes are engraved along the sheath. Overall length 11½ ins. Blade 8⅕ ins. (2) Ivory hilt with fairly wide crossguard and a pommel cap in form of an embossed lion's head. The blade is engraved with simple floral motif. Overall length 12⅖ ins. Blade 9 ins. (3) Ivory and gilt hilt with swelling cap embossed with a beehive. The blade blued and gilt. A metal sheath is engraved with simple floral motif. Overall length 13$\frac{7}{10}$ ins. Blade 9 ins. (4) Stiff, skewer-like blade with circular guard and metal scabbard. Overall length 12 ins. Blade 8⅘ ins. All are probably English and date from late 18th/early 19th cent.

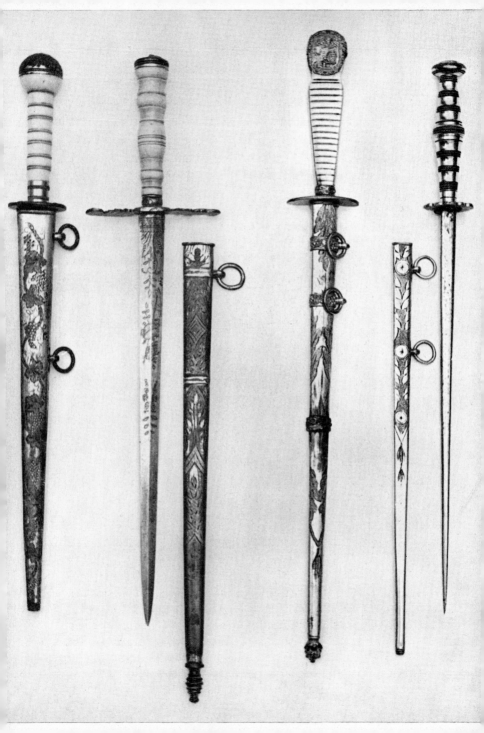

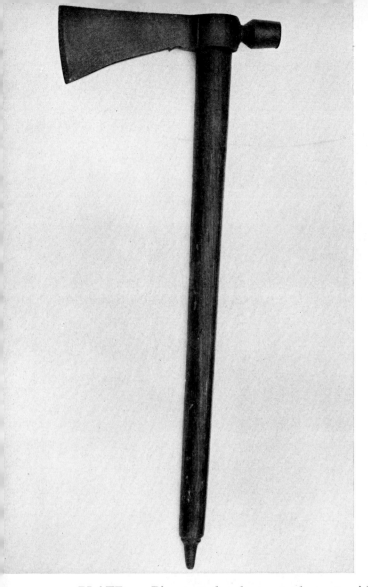

PLATE 122 Pipe tomahawk stamped on one side of blade with name of maker HOLTZAPPFEL and on the other the broad arrow and letters B.O.—Board of Ordnance. Such tomahawks were used for trading and presentation to the Red Indian tribes and symbolised both peace—the pipe—and war. The haft is pierced and the end shaped to form a mouthpiece. Haft length 21¾ ins. Height of head (overall) 9⅕ ins. English. Circa 1810.

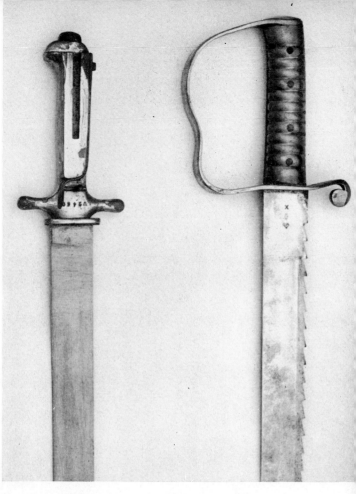

PLATE 123 *Left:* Brass-hilted Prussian bayonet—*hirsch-fanger*—with a fitting designed to slide over and lock on to a lug at the side of barrel. Carried in a black leather sheath with brass fittings. Overall length 23⅞ ins. Blade 18¾ ins. Prussian early 19th century. *Right:* Brass-hilted Infantry Pioneer sword of 1856 pattern made by WILKINSON, LONDON. A saw back was intended to make weapon serve also as a tool. This model was withdrawn from service in 1903 and passed to Royal Navy to be used as cutlasses. Overall length 27 ins. Blade 22½ ins. Made in England, 1898.

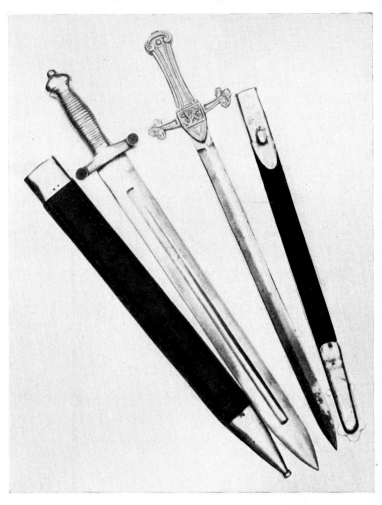

PLATE 124 *Left:* Broadly based on the Roman *gladius* this type of sword was very popular in many European countries around the middle of the 19th century. Hilts were usually of brass, commonly ridged like this one, or cast in a variety of bird's heads. Most sheaths are of black leather with brass fittings. Overall length $25\frac{3}{10}$ ins. Blade $19\frac{1}{2}$ ins. Austrian (?), about 1840. *Right:* Later style of band sword with cast-brass hilt and rather inefficient blades, a matter of little importance since they were purely decorative. Overall length $24\frac{1}{2}$ ins. Blade $18\frac{1}{2}$ ins. English. Circa 1850.

PLATE 125 Scottish broadsword or claymore carried by Lt.-
Col. E. J. Elliott of 79th Foot Cameron Highlanders who died
at Varna during the Crimean War. A red fringe decorates
the pommel. Overall length 37 ins. Blade 31¾ ins.
Scottish, about 1850.

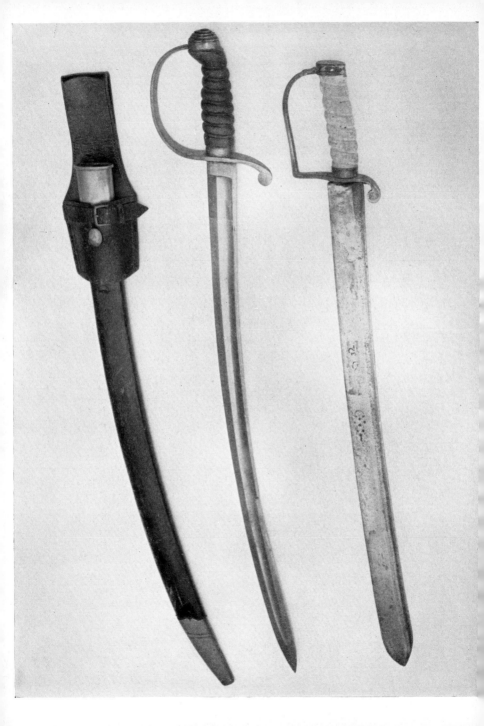

PLATE 126 *Left:* Typical hanger carried by some police, prison warders or kept for personal protection. Many have spring clips locking them into the scabbard of black leather. Hilts and scabbard mounts may be of brass or steel. Overall length 27 ins. Blade 22¼ ins. English. Circa 1850. *Right:* Interesting example of rehilted blade, for the hilt is late 18th century in style whilst the blade is late 16th or early 17th century and has obviously been cut down. Overall length 27½ ins. Blade 22⅗ ins. English hilt 18th century.

PLATE 127 *Left:* Hilt of *shamshir* or sabre with a horn grip and silver decoration. The Duke of Wellington is supposed to have made this style popular and it was officially adopted for General Officers in 1831, and called the Mameluke hilt. Overall length 39½ ins. Blade 33½ ins. Turkish or Egyptian 17th century. *Right:* Victorian florid Mameluke hilt with ivory grip and very elaborate sheath. (See plates 129 and 130.)

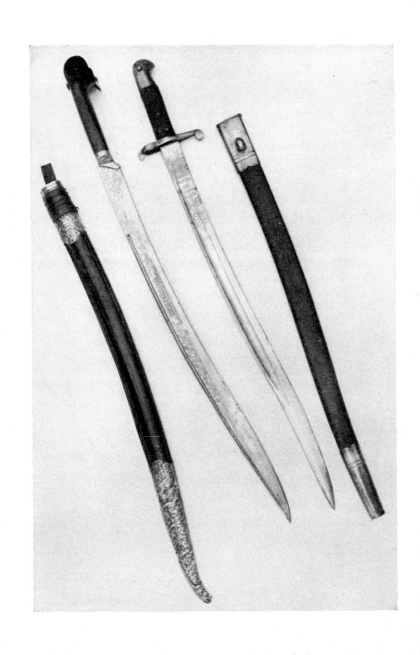

PLATE 128 *Left:* This *yataghan* has two large ears and a grip of horn decorated with three square brass rivets whilst the blade is decorated with typical silver damascening. The scabbard is of leather-covered wood with brass locket and chape. Overall length 28½ ins. Blade 22¾ ins. Balkan 19th century. *Right: Yataghan* bayonet by PARKER FIELD of London. The shape of the blade is very similar to that of the true *yataghan* and was commonly used by many European armies of this period. Scabbard of black leather with steel mounts. Overall length 28 ins. Blade 22¼ ins. English. Circa 1860.

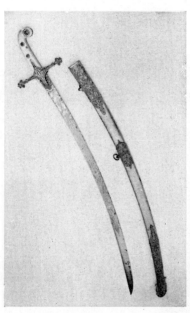

PLATE 129 & 130 A presentation sword with ivory grip, gilt brass quillons and scabbard. The curved blade is deeply etched with a dedication. Sword was made by HAWKES & CO. LONDON. Overall length 35¾ ins. Blade 30½ ins. English. 1856.

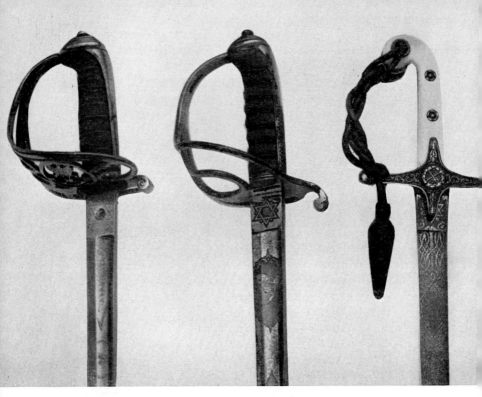

PLATE 131 *Left:* **Rifle Brigade sword of pattern used from
1834 to 1895. Set in the steel guard is the horn which
is the badge of the Rifle Brigade. Overall length 38 ins.
Blade 32½ ins. English. Circa 1860.** *Centre:* **Royal Artillery sword presented to Sir E. H. Elliott, Senior Executive
Officer of Queen's Bodyguard of Yeomen of Guard. The blade
is etched with Elliott crest and motto. Overall length 40½
ins. Blade 34½ ins. English. 1875.** *Right:* **Mameluke sword
of 1831 pattern by E. THURKLE MAKER SOHO, LONDON.
The sword knot is red and silver and fits through an ivory grip
whilst the slightly curved blade is etched with patterns.
Overall length 37 ins. Blade 31½ ins. English. Circa 1860.**

PLATE 132 Hunting knives with horn grips, plain cross-guards and silver mounts. The one on the left is unmarked but has silver-mounted sheath with simple gilded decoration. That on the right is stamped FENN on the blade and has steel mounts on the sheath. *Left:* overall length $11\frac{13}{16}$ ins. Blade $7\frac{1}{2}$ ins. English. Circa 1850. *Right:* overall length $17\frac{1}{4}$ ins. Blade 12 ins. English (?) Circa 1850.

PLATE 133 This fearsome looking knife is one of a group known as Green River knives after those originally manufactured at Green River, Greenfield, Massachusetts. Sheffield cutlers copied the style and this specimen is marked with a crown and V. R. UNWIN & RODGERS, CUTLERS, SHEF-FIELD. Overall length 13⅞ ins. Blade 9 ins. English. Circa 1860.

PLATE 134 *From left to right:* (1) Victorian hunting knife, with silver hilt and blade stamped with a crown and VR and CAST STEEL. Overall length 12⅘ ins. Blade 8⅕ ins. English. Circa 1860. (2) Peasant knife from Southern Europe with bone grip embellished with small brass studs. Overall length 13 ins. Blade 8 ins. Spanish or Italian. Early 19th century. (3) Peasant dagger fitted with curved quill-ons. Hilt of wood and brass. Overall length 11½ ins. Blade 7⅕ ins. Italian (?) 19th cent-ury. (4) Macabre knife inscribed W & S BUTCHERS SPORTSMAN KNIFE with bone grip fashioned in shape of a coffin complete with plaque on lid. Overall length 10½ ins. Blade 6 ins. English. Late 19th century.

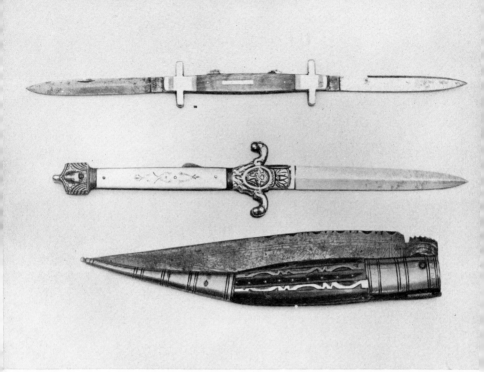

PLATE 135 *Top to bottom:* (1) An unusual double-bladed knife designed to provide protection against the garotter who crept up behind and strangled his victim. On one blade is stamped ANTI-GAROTTE and on the other UNWIN & RODGERS SHEFFIELD. Overall length open $13\frac{7}{8}$ ins. Each blade $4\frac{1}{2}$ ins. English. Circa 1860. (2) Fine folding knife with mother-of-pearl grips. A small projection set at the side of the grip has to be pressed to unlock the blade for closing. Overall length open 13 ins. Blade $5\frac{7}{10}$ ins. English (?). Circa 1850. (3) Large Spanish knife with brass-decorated handle and an etched blade bearing a motto and the date 1878. The blade is locked into position by a strong spring engaging in the notches at the rear of the blade. Overall length open 21 ins. Blade 10 ins. Made in Spain in about 1878.

PLATE 136 *Top to bottom:* (1) Spanish knife dated 1878 (see
Plate 135). (2) Spanish knife fitted with various accessories for the gun—a screwdriver, pricker to clean the
touch hole, and, at the end of the grip, a nipple key.
Overall length open $14\frac{9}{10}$ ins. Blade $6\frac{9}{10}$ ins. Spanish
19th century. (3) Good quality Spanish knife, blade etched
VIVA LA REPUBLICA, the handle of tortoiseshell and
mother-of-pearl. Overall length open $15\frac{3}{5}$ ins. Blade $7\frac{3}{5}$ ins.
Made in Spain in about 1870.

PLATE 137 Dirk of Argyll and Sutherland Highlanders with silver mounts and large stones set in the hilts of both implements and dirk. Interest in these weapons was revived by the romantic novels of Sir Walter Scott and Royal visits to Scotland early in the 19th century. Blade length $11\frac{1}{2}$ ins. Scottish. Circa 1900.

PLATE 138 *Left:* Midshipman's dirk, blade etched with strapwork, fouled anchor and Royal Arms. When the dirk was pushed into its scabbard a slot in the quillon engaged with a spring clip projecting above the mouth of the scabbard so locking the weapon into place. Overall length 23¼ ins. Blade 18⅛ ins. English, 1890. *Right:* Fine clean example of naval dress sword with brass guard, the side section of which folds down and engages with a stud on the locket so holding the sword in the scabbard. The hilt has a lion's head pommel and a sword knot of 1891 pattern. Overall length 37½ ins. Blade 31½ ins. Made in England about 1930 (?).

PLATE 140 Cruciform hilt typical of so many swords used as part of their regalia by societies and organisations. Theatrical swords were often made in the same style and very few of this type have any identifying marks at all. Overall length 36 ins. Blade $29\frac{3}{4}$ ins. Late 19th century (?).

PLATE 139 *Left:* Fine bowie knife made in Sheffield with mounts of silver embossed with U.S. Eagle and shield. Mother-of-pearl strips decorate the hilt and the blade is etched with patterns and GOLD SEEKERS PROTECTOR. On the *ricasso* is stamped JOHN LINGARD'S CELEBRATED BOWIE KNIFE PEACROFT. A red leather sheath is decorated with a simple gilt pattern. Overall length $13\frac{2}{5}$ ins. Blade $8\frac{2}{5}$ ins. English. Circa 1860. *Centre:* Bowie of much plainer, more workmanlike style. The hilt is of plain wood and the blade is substantial but bears no marks at all. A plain crossguard of brass has two bulbous terminals. Overall length $13\frac{9}{10}$ ins. Blade 9 ins. U.S. (?). Circa 1850. *Left:* A bowie plug bayonet which may well have been made by some trapper or hunter seeking a double purpose weapon. A letter T is deeply stamped on to the blade. The crossguard is of brass. Overall length $14\frac{3}{10}$ ins. Blade $9\frac{1}{2}$ ins. U.S.A. (?). Circa 1860 (?).

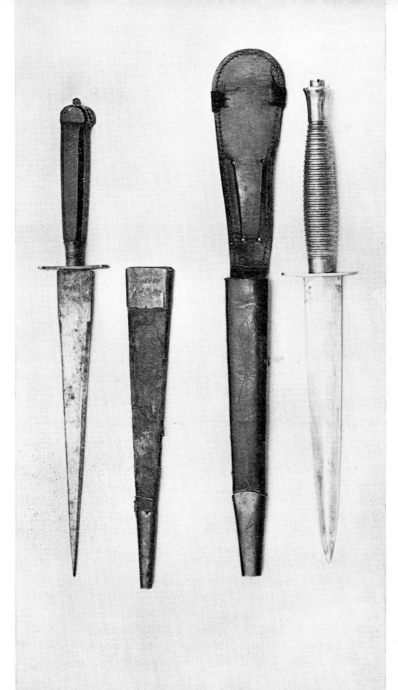

PLATE 141 *Left:* Simple dagger with black horn grip, simple brass crossguard and black leather sheath. The locket is inscribed AJACCIO SEPRE 1832. Overall length 12 ins. Blade $7\frac{7}{10}$ ins. Corsican 1832. *Right:* Designed for the British Commando, this fighting knife has a black, cast-metal hilt and slim double-edged blade. Overall length $11\frac{3}{5}$ ins. Blade $6\frac{9}{10}$ ins. British. Circa 1940.

PLATE 142 This officer's sword of the Imperial German Navy has very fine damascus blade etched with fouled anchors, sailing ships, steam ships and similar nautical motifs. Even the lion's head pommel has red and green eyes appropriately positioned on port and starboard! Overall length 36 ins. Blade $30\frac{1}{2}$ ins. German. Pre-1918.

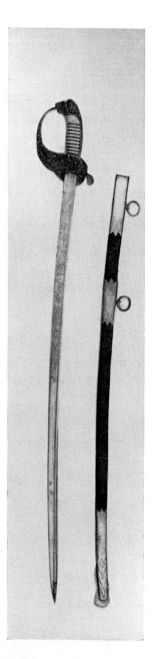

PLATE 143 *Left to Right:* (1) 1871 pattern bayonet for the Mauser rifle with double curved quillons and brass hilt. Overall length 23⅝ ins. Blade 18½ ins. German post-1875. (2) Mauser bayonet, pattern of 1898, with single short quillon and narrow straight blade. Overall length 25⅝ ins. Blade 20½ ins. German. Circa 1900. (3) A blade which widened towards the point earned for this weapon the name Mauser Butcher bayonet. Overall length 19½ ins. Blade 14½ ins. German. 1914/18.

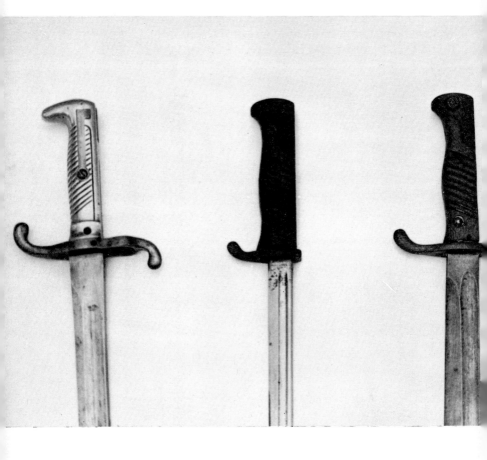

PLATE 144 *Left to right:* (1) The blade of this Lebel bayonet was cruciform in section since four deep grooves were cut into a circular block. Earlier models have a curly quillon which was discarded in 1916. Overall length 25 ins. Blade 20 ins. French. Post-1916. (2) In 1907 a sword bayonet with a curly quillon was adopted for the Lee Enfield rifle. This quillon was discontinued on later models to produce the type here illustrated which continued to do service during the Second World War. Overall length 22 ins. Blade $17\frac{1}{4}$ ins. English 1917. (3) Rather short, but nicely proportioned, this was the bayonet for the Lee Metford rifle. Overall length $16\frac{7}{8}$ ins. Blade 12 ins. English. Circa 1890.

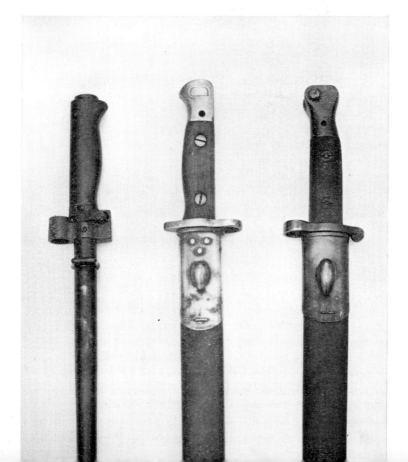

PLATE 145 Designed by a committee which had tested a
variety of swords, the pattern of 1908 was, in effect, the
last British cavalry sword designed for action. It was
decided that ideally the cavalry needed a thrusting
weapon and the blade was consequently long and stiff. A
very comfortable grip was protected by a very large,
solid shellguard. The scabbard was of steel with two
large carrying rings. Overall length 42½ ins. Blade
35 ins. British. 1908 pattern.

PLATE 146 Folding trench knife with its leather sheath
fitted at the back with a loop to fasten it to a belt.
When folded the weapon is $8\frac{3}{5}$ ins. long, but when fully
opened locks the blade and crossguard into position.
To close the blade it must be first unlocked by pressing
the metal stud visible in the grip. Overall length open
12 ins. Blade $7\frac{7}{10}$ ins. German 1914/18.

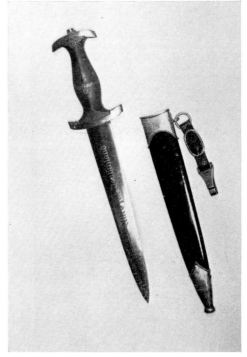

PLATES 147 & 148 Dagger and sheath of N.S.K.K. or Motor
Transport Corps differing from that of the S.A. by having
a black sheath. Reference to plate 33 will soon make
clear how closely the Nazis copied the Holbein daggers.
Etched on the spear blade is the motto ALLES FUR DEUTSH-
LAND (All for Germany) and it is also stamped SOLINGEN.
The light brown wooden grip is set with the sign of the
S.A. and a swastika and eagle. Overall length $12\frac{4}{5}$ ins.
Blade $8\frac{4}{5}$ ins. German. Post-1934.

PLATE 149 The N.S.K.K. Leader's dagger, essentially the same as that in plate 148 except for the elaborate suspension chain with its eagle and swastika links.

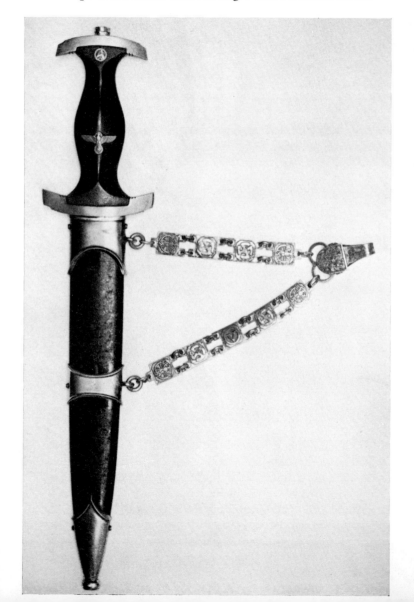

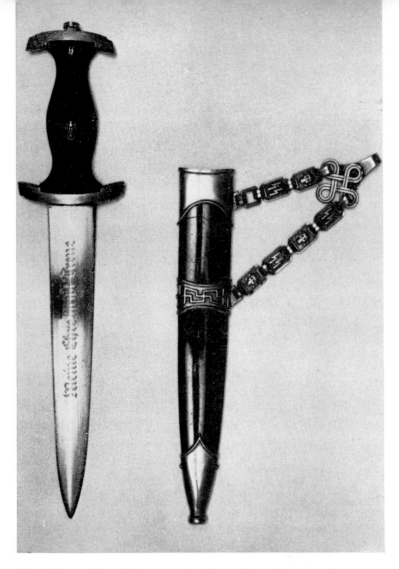

PLATE 150 The S.S. were the élite of the German forces
and this is the 1936 pattern dagger of an S.S. officer
with blade engraved MEINE EHRE HEISST TREUE (My
honour is loyalty). The chain is composed of links with
the skull and crossbones and the symbol of the S.S. The
main difference between the S.S. and S.A. daggers was
in the colour of the grip—black for the S.S. and brown
for the S.A. Overall length 12⅘ ins. Blade 8⅘ ins. Made
in Germany after 1934.

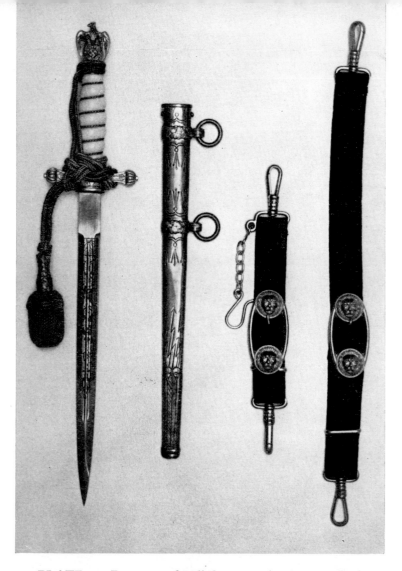

PLATE 151 Daggers of a different style were made for
officers of the German armed forces and this is the 1938
Naval pattern differing from earlier models mainly in
the style of pommel. At least two common styles of
scabbards were in use. This model is complete with its
carrying straps. Blade length $9\frac{7}{8}$ ins. German. Post-1938.

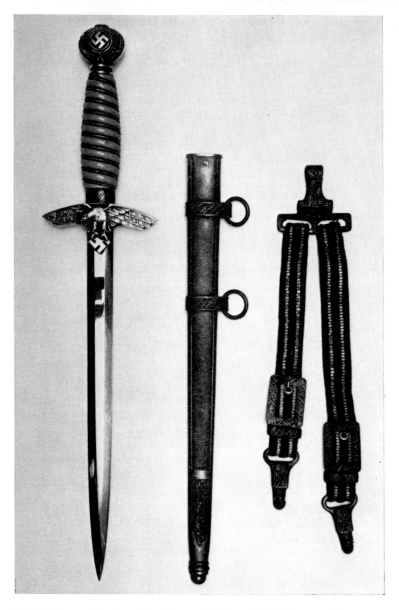

PLATE 152 For the Air Force (Luftwaffe) Officers this
pattern was introduced in 1937. It had a plastic grip
of various colours ranging from orange to white. Blade
length $10\frac{1}{4}$ ins. German. Post-1937.

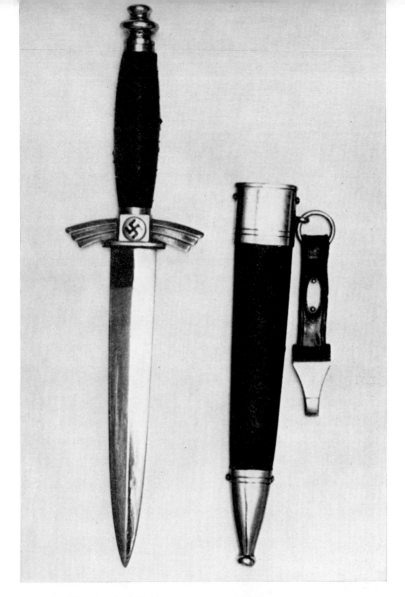

PLATE 153 Realising the importance of air power the Nazis stimulated every interest in flying and formed the Nationalsozialistische Fliegerkorps N.S.F.K. This dagger was designed in 1934 for use by all members and had a blue leather grip and scabbard. Overall length 13½ ins. Blade 6⅞ ins. German. Post-1934.

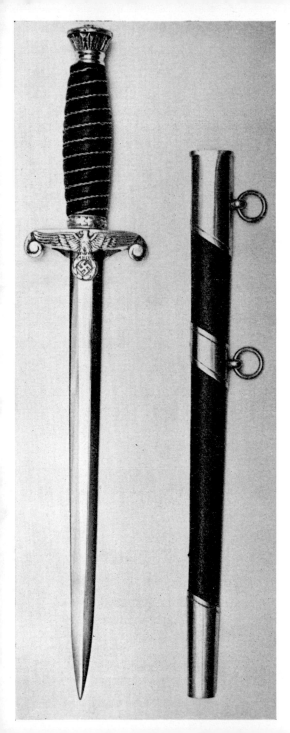

PLATE 154 Even non-military groups such as the Customs were issued with a dagger which was very similar to that of the army. This is the type carried by the Land Customs and has a green grip and scabbard with silver finished metal fittings. Overall length $16\frac{1}{8}$ ins. Blade $10\frac{1}{4}$ ins. German. Post-1934.

PLATE 155 German police had issue bayonets and this is the model carried during the period of the Weimar Republic and is distinguished by the shell bearing the eagle of the Republic which is also set in the grip. These bayonets were also made in parade styles which lacked means of attaching them to a rifle. Blade length $9\frac{7}{8}$ ins. German. Pre-1933.

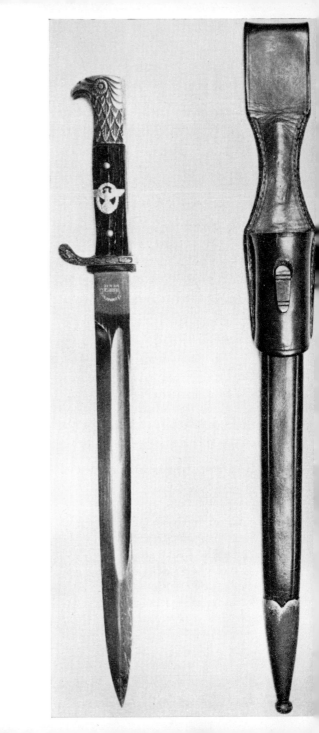

PLATE 156 When the Nazis took over, existing bayonets were either adapted or replaced, and in the case of the police the Nazi emblem replaced the eagle of Weimar and the shell was discarded. Black scabbards were used by regular police whilst those of the *gendarmerie* were brown. Blade length 9⅞ ins. German. Post-1934.

PLATE 157 At first glance a nice early 19th-century officer's small-sword, but a closer look raises a number of queries. The pommel, knuckle and bow and shells are not quite right, although the entire hilt is of good quality. If the weapon is drawn from its sheath it is immediately obvious that this is not a weapon. Made in Germany for the theatre it is just possible that it might deceive a new collector. Overall length 34 ins. Blade length 28 ins. Made in Germany in 1960.

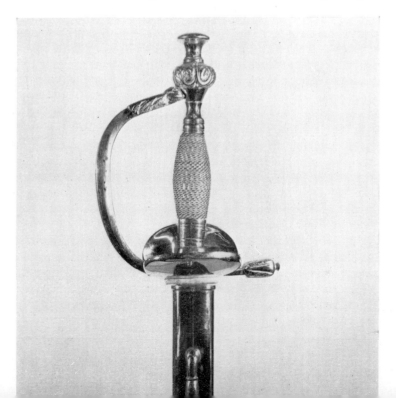

ORIENTAL WEAPONS

If the range of European weapons is large that of the Orient, with its variety of styles, size and quality, is enormous. The position is further complicated by a complete lack of discernible pattern of development in the majority of weapons. Research and publication of material on the weapons of Asia and Africa have lagged far behind that on European items. Collectors will find that so often it is extremely difficult to identify a piece with any great precision.

Dating is very difficult indeed and only when a piece can be dated on reasonably good grounds have any figures been given in the captions. It is extremely likely that the great majority of these weapons are, in fact, 19th century, made when Britain's empire was expanding rapidly. Many homecoming travellers brought with them the souvenirs which they had purchased from the local market or tribe. However, amongst this great mass of material there were some older weapons, and enough to make it unwise to put a blanket date of 19th century on all such souvenirs.

On the whole, the quality of the Asiatic weapons illustrated is good since, all else being equal, there is a more plentiful supply of good pieces available for the collector in this field.

The photographs are grouped on a regional basis—Indonesia, Africa, India, China and Japan.

PLATE 158 *Top:* Straight-bladed *kris* from Java with characteristic slightly curved grip. Although no two are quite identical the sheath with its upcurving point is very typical of Javanese *kris*. Overall length 18½ ins. Blade 14 ins. Javanese. *Bottom:* Known as a kingfisher *kris* the hilt has, in fact, nothing to do with this bird and the long, thin spike has an animal or demon connotation. The straight blade has a hair-like watered pattern. Overall length 20 ins. Blade 16³⁄₁₀ ins. Malayan from Patani on the North coast.

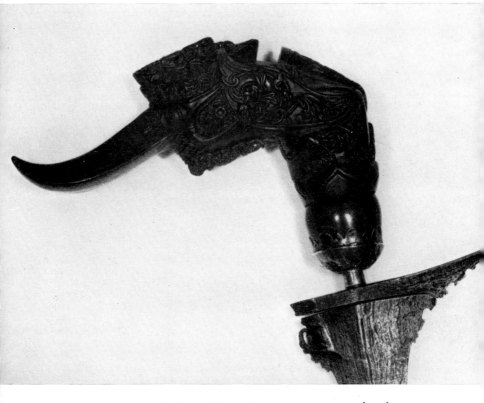

PLATE 159 Detail of the grip (plate 158) showing intricate carving of tracery. Length of nose $2\frac{1}{2}$ ins.

PLATE 160 *Jambiya* with a sheath of exaggerated proportion. The long silver chape stands some $10\frac{1}{2}$ ins. high, but its sole purpose is decorative and the sheath and belt are of poor quality, hardly warranting such elaborate decoration. Silver studs and sheet decorate the hilt. Overall length $11\frac{1}{2}$ ins. Blade $7\frac{1}{5}$ ins. From the Gulf of Oman. 19th century.

PLATE 162 Detail from *Jambiya* in plate 161 left, showing the hilt and gold inlay at the top of the blade.

PLATE 161 *Left:* A variant of the *Jambiya* which lacks
certain common features such as a central rib on the
blade and a curled edge to the scabbard. Embossed
silver covers the sheath and hilt and the top section
of the blade is gold inlaid. Overall length 18 ins.
Blade 12⅖ ins. Arabia (Wahabite) 19th century (?).
Right: Slightly more characteristic is this Balkan
Jambiya since the blade is ribbed. Silver decoration
is used on the sheath and on the bone grip. Overall
length 16½ ins. Blade 10½ ins. Albanian. 19th century.

PLATE 163 At first glance not unlike the early Viking
swords this is, in fact, a *Tuareg* sword from North Africa.
A wide blade, $2\frac{1}{4}$ ins., has no less than five fullers
whilst the leather grip is covered with sheet brass
with raised patterns of punched dots. It is rare to
find such weapons retaining their leather sword knots.
Overall length $39\frac{7}{8}$ ins. Blade $34\frac{1}{4}$ ins. Made in North
Africa in the 19th century.

PLATE 164 Hilt of Sudanese or *Hausa* sword with leather covered grip, disc pommel, and straight, slightly flaring quillons with long langets to grip the top of the scabbard. The blade is straight and double edged and engraved with a design of sun, moon and stars and a long quotation from the Koran. A large number of these swords are fitted with European-made blades. Overall length 38¾ ins. Blade 33¼ ins. Sudanese. 18th century.

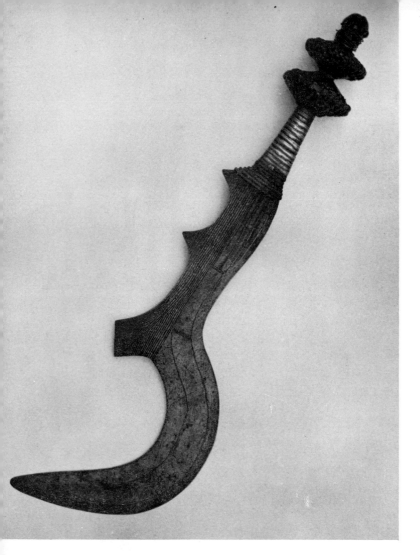

PLATE 165 Sickle-like sword from the Congo, the hilt decorated with narrow brass strip wire and round-headed tacks. It is single edged with the cutting edge on the outside of the curved section. Overall length 25 ins. Blade 16½ ins.

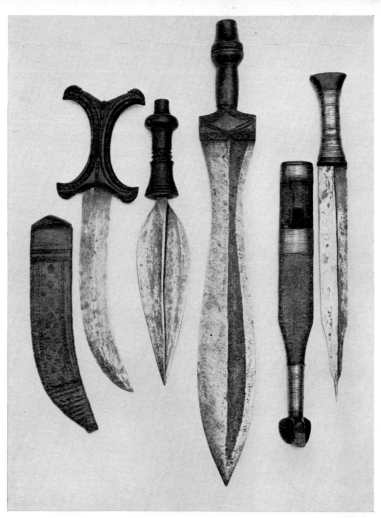

PLATE 166 (1) Common type of Somali or Sudanese dagger
with the characteristic X-shaped grip, curving blade,
and leather sheath. Overall length 11⅖ ins. Blade
7⁹⁄₁₀ ins. Sudanese. Late 19th century. (2) Spear-bladed
knife with prominent central rib and plain wooden grip.
Overall length 11⅖ ins. Blade 7⅖ ins. Congo (?).
(3) Leaf-bladed sword very reminiscent in shape of
Bronze Age weapons. Overall length 25 ins. Blade
20 ins. Congo. (4) Scabbard and grip are of wood bound
with brass wire. The blade tapers to a needle point
in the same fashion as a group of Bronze Age swords.
Overall length 13³⁄₁₀ ins. Blade 10 ins. M'Chona, Africa.

PLATE 167 Three African spears. The centre spearhead and ferrule are typical of Masai spears although there are variations in design. The spear on the right has been bound with a thick metal strip and wire to give it extra weight for penetrating power. Kenya.

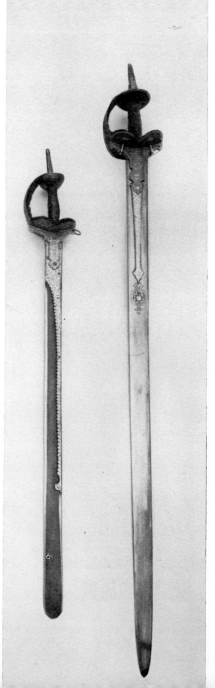

PLATE 168 *Right: Khandars*
are more or less the eq-
ivalent of the European
hand-and-a-half swords
for the projecting spike
enables a two-handed grip
to be used if desired.
Langets help to stiffen
the blade which is of
Indian manufacture but in
the European style. The
padding survives in the
guard and around the grip.
Overall length 44½ ins.
Blade 38 ins. Indian
18th century. *Left:* A
small *Khandar* for a boy
with rich gold inlay and
a blade with the typical
widening towards the point.
Again the watered blade is
strengthened by the bar
at the back. Overall
length 34⅜ ins. Blade
27½ ins. Made in India
in late 18th century.

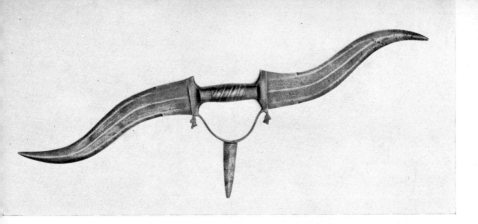

PLATE 169 Held by the bar at the centre this all-metal parrying knife was probably nearly as dangerous to defender as to attacker. Overall length 26½ ins. Indian.

PLATE 170 Tiger claws—*bagh nakh*—for the right hand since the larger (thumb) ring is to the right. A varying number of claws may be fitted to the bar and many, like this, are decorated with silver damascening. Plate 3⅕ ins. Claws 1½ ins. Indian. 19th century.

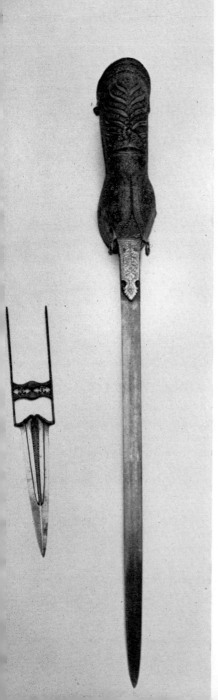

PLATE 171 *Left: Katar* or punch dagger with finely chiselled steel blade. In common with a large number of these weapons the point is thickened to assist in penetrating mail. The sheath is covered with green velvet. Overall length 17⅝ ins. Blade 9¼ ins. Indian. *Right: Pata*—gauntlet sword— with the gauntlet decorated with silver damascening and two projecting tigers' heads with ruby eyes. This weapon is unique in having a hinged flat which covers the lower side of the gauntlet. Overall length 43 ins. Blade 30½ ins. Indian. 17th century.

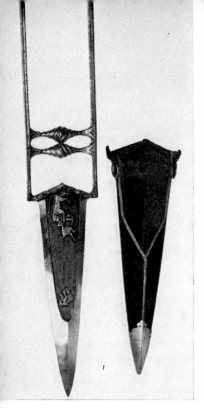

PLATES 172 & 173 Another *katar* of very high quality with watered blade inlaid with gold and chiselled with the popular motif of a leopard attacking a deer. The sheath is covered with purple velvet and has two rings at the mouth for suspension at the belt. Overall length $17\frac{1}{2}$ ins. Blade $8\frac{4}{5}$ ins. Indian. 18th century.

PLATE 174 Superb quality axe of steel covered with gold damascening. The head of the deer has two small rubies inset for eyes and the tongue is made separately and set into the mouth. Overall length $25\frac{1}{4}$ ins. Haft 22 ins. Mogul. Made in the 17th century.

PLATE 175 *Left:* Very typical in its form, with T-sect-
ion blade, and "step" below the grip, is this *pesh kabz*
with its dark green mineral grip and green velvet covered sheath. Overall length 14½ ins. Blade 10 ins.
North India. 19th century. *Centre: Pesh kabz* with a
common form of sheath in which the hilt sits well into
the mouth—a style often found with Afghan or Khyber
knives. The hilt is of ivory and scabbard is of wood
covered with leather. Overall length 17⅛ ins. Blade
11⅜ ins. Northern India. *Right:* Not all *pesh kabz* are
straight and a number have blades with varying degrees
of curve. Many also have reinforced points for mail
piercing. Length 13⁷⁄₁₀ ins. Blade 9 ins. N. Indian.

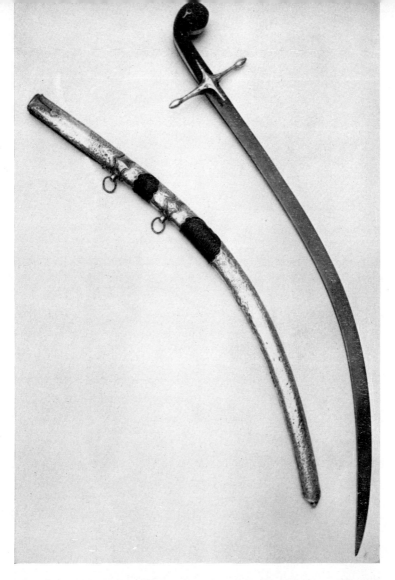

PLATE 176 A leather sheath, almost entirely covered with
embossed silver, has the back split to facilitate
the drawing of the long curved blade. The blade is
Persian and is unusual in that it carries three sig-
natures. A grip of buffalo horn is in the Turkish form
decorated with silver and is later in date than the
blade. Overall length $40\frac{1}{2}$ ins. Blade $34\frac{1}{2}$ ins.
Turkish or Egyptian. 18th century manufacture.

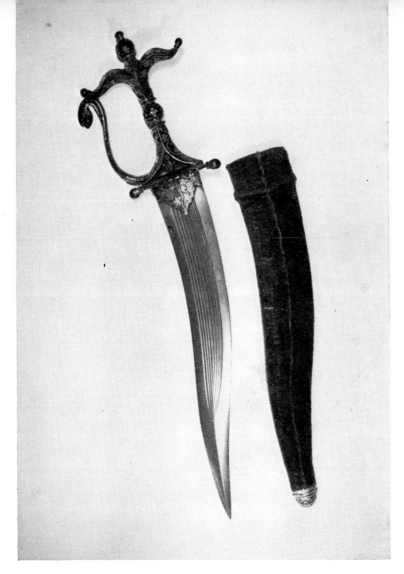

PLATE 177 All-metal, double-curved dagger with inlaid
hilt with its red velvet covered sheath and gold tipped
chape. This type of dagger is called a *chilanum*. Overall length 15 ins. Blade $11\frac{1}{10}$ ins. Mahratta.

PLATE 178 *Talwar* with sheath and baldric or sling, which, although only associated, is of correct type and style. Decorated with gold and silver and on the blade an invocation to both Allah and Alli. Overall length 36 ins. Blade 31½ ins. Indian. Late 18th century.

PLATE 179 *Left:* Dagger with light grey-green-jade hilt
carved overall with a floral motif and with down-turned
quillons. Gold thread embellishes the brocaded sheath.
Overall length 14½ ins. Blade 9½ ins. 17th century (?)
Right: Similar, also with a jade hilt in bold style.
Both blades have thickened points. Overall length 15 ins.
Blade 10 ins. Late 17th or 18th century.

PLATE 180 Large-sized *talwar* with wide blade, $3\frac{3}{10}$ ins. at its widest, embossed with trees, mosques, lions and elephants. Pommel and grip are also embossed with floral pattern and a sunburst. This ceremonial weapon weighs 3 lbs. 10 ozs. Overall length 31 ins. Blade 24 ins. Made in Southern India.

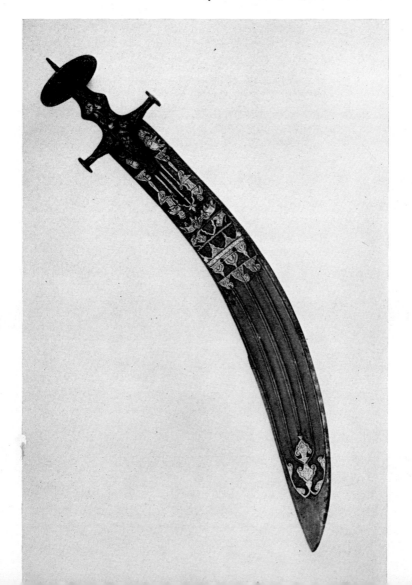

PLATE 182 *Left: Talwar* with a guard of three bars and bulbous pommel, both unusual features. The steel is inlaid with floral patterns in gold. Overall length 37¾ ins. Blade 32½ ins. Sikh. Early 18th century. *Centre: Talwar* with a very characteristic hilt shape. Sheath mounts are gilt and the hilt is inlaid with gold and fitted with a fine native-made watered blade. Overall length 36 ins. Blade 30¼ ins. Persian. *Right:* Late 18th century Indian *talwar* (see plate 178).

PLATE 181 *Left:* Enamel-inlaid hilt of a *shamshir* with tiger heads at pommel and quillon ends and fine damascus Khorassan blade. Overall length 36 ins. Blade 31 ins. Indian 18th century. *Centre:* Hilt and scabbard mounts of *niello* silver and exhibiting signs of European influence in having a locket which is unusual on Persian swords. Blade signed and dated. Overall length 39 ins. Blade 33½ ins. Persian. 1749. *Right:* Walrus ivory has been combined with enamel in this hilt, the pommel in the shape of the head of a Persian dragon. The blade is Persian. Length 38½ ins. Blade 33 ins. 18th century.

PLATE 183 Dagger—*piha-kaetta*—from Ceylon with silver sheath and hilt. Many of these knives also have a stylus fitted in the sheath. Overall length 10 ins. Made in Ceylon in the 18th (?) century.

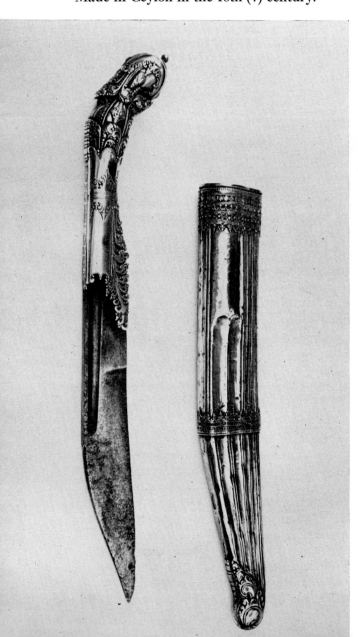

PLATE 184 Known variously as *kindjal* or *qama*, these
weapons were popular in much of Russia, Persia and
the Balkans. The long, heavy, straight blade is double edged
with a very deep fuller and is not unlike the Roman *gladius*
in shape. This particular sheath retains its original belt
and decorative tassel. Overall length 30 ins. Blade $23\frac{1}{2}$
ins. Made in the Caucasus in the 19th century.

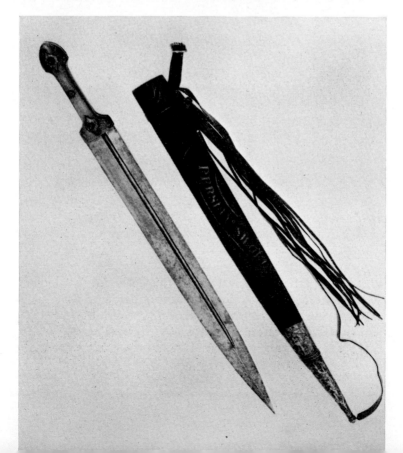

PLATE 185 Often associated with the Cossacks, this long sword—*shashqa*—has a slightly curving blade (in this case bearing the Solingen mark) and typical hilt. Sword and sheath are decorated with silver. Overall length 36 ins. Blade 29⅜ ins. Caucasus. 19th century, blade earlier.

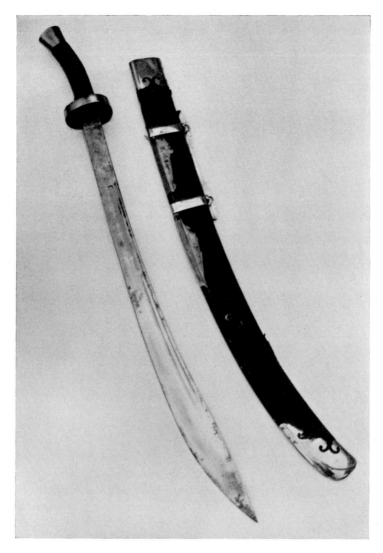

PLATE 186 An executioner's two-handed sword from China
of better quality than usual. The widening blade is
engraved with a dragon. Overall length 39 ins. Blade
31 ins. Chinese. Late 19th century.

PLATE 187 *Left:* Small *aikuchi*—a dagger without a
guard. A corrugated sheath has a slot which holds a
smaller knife called a *kozuka*. Overall length $13\frac{1}{10}$ ins.
Blade $9\frac{1}{2}$ ins. Japanese. *Right:* A short sword—*wakizashi*
—with the mounts signed by OMORI TERUHIDE.
A dragon decorates the lacquered sheath which also has
its *kozuka*. Overall length $22\frac{4}{5}$ ins. Blade 16 ins. Made
in Japan in the 18th century.

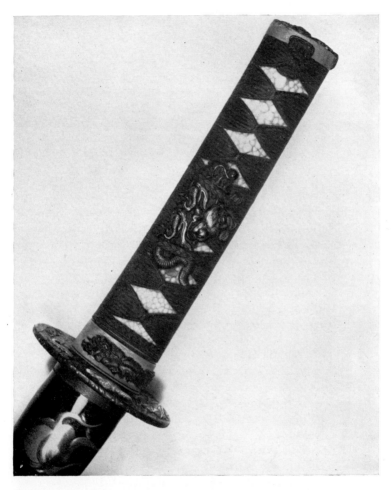

PLATE 188 Hilt of the *wakizashi* (see plate 187) showing
the *menuki* (the small ornaments underneath the binding)
fashioned like dragons, a motif repeated on the *tsuba*
and bottom mount *(fuchi)*. Length of hilt 6⅘ ins.

PLATE 189 *Top left:* Unsigned *tsuba* with birds in flight.
School of Kinai, Echizen Province, early 18th century.
3 ins. diam. by $2\frac{3}{4}$ ins. *Top right:* Unsigned *tsuba* with
Samurai warriors. Otsuki school of Kyōto Province, mid-
19th century. $2\frac{7}{10}$ ins. by $2\frac{2}{5}$ ins. *Bottom:* Large signed
tsuba with some copper inlay. The inscription gives the
name of the maker (Sōten), his town (Hikone), and province (Ōmi). $3\frac{2}{5}$ ins. by $3\frac{1}{10}$ ins. About 1720.

PLATES 190 and 191 *Left:* Probably the most common of
   all Japanese swords is this army officer's pattern. The
scabbard was of wood or metal, but in combat was covered
   with brown leather. A large number of blades were fact-
      ory made between 1939 and 1945, but this particular
blade is signed KANE YOSNI and is probably 16th century.
   The colour of the sword knot indicates the grade of off-
      icer. Blue for company, red for field, and red and gold
         for generals. *Right:* A similar naval officer's sword
         but with a scabbard of dark blue sharkskin with two
            carrying rings. This blade has been shortened, but it
                  appears to be an early one.

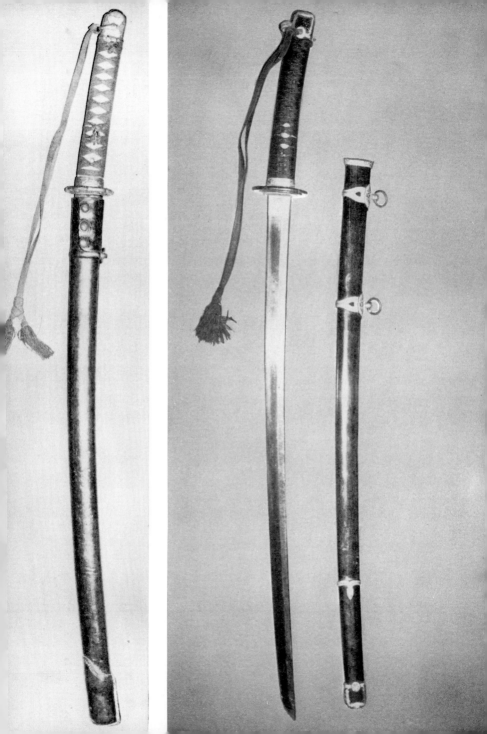

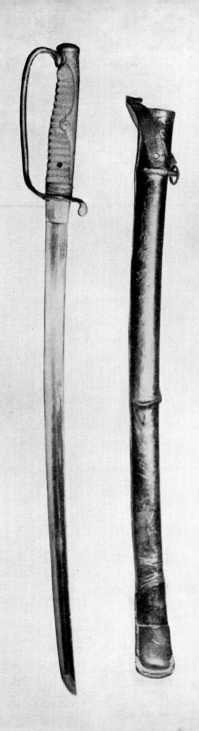

PLATE 192 European influence is apparent in the style of hilt with its knucklebow which is not usual on Japanese swords. Swords mounted in this fashion are described as KYU-GUNTO (Proto Army), and were popular at turn of century.
Scabbards were chromium, plated but were covered with leather. This specimen has a blade signed NO KAMI FUJI WARA NO NOBU YOSHI. Circa 1670–80.

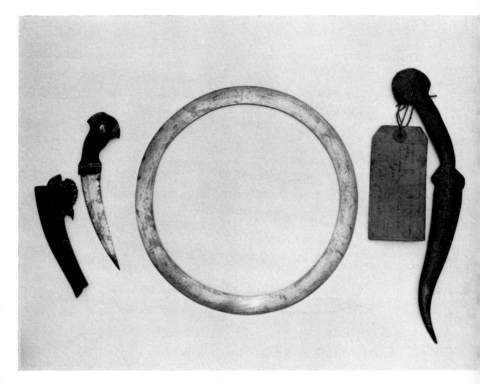

PLATE 193 *Left:* Small Indonesian parrot dagger with
blackwood sheath and matching hilt with detail lined in
white. Overall length $6\frac{1}{2}$ ins. Blade $4\frac{1}{10}$ ins.
Centre: Chakram or steel quoit used by the Sikhs. Diam.
$9\frac{3}{10}$ ins. *Right:* Rare Indian horn dagger still retaining its original auction sale label of 1915—price
two shillings! Overall length $10\frac{1}{2}$ ins. Blade 6 ins.

PLATE 194 *Left:* Scissors dagger, the "hilt" decorated with coral and inlay. The green velvet sheath is also decorated in the same style. Overall length 12 ins. Blade (to axis) $6\frac{4}{5}$ ins. Middle East (?). *Right:* "T" dagger with leather-bound grip. Overall length $10\frac{2}{5}$ ins. Blade $7\frac{7}{10}$ ins. Made in Africa (?).

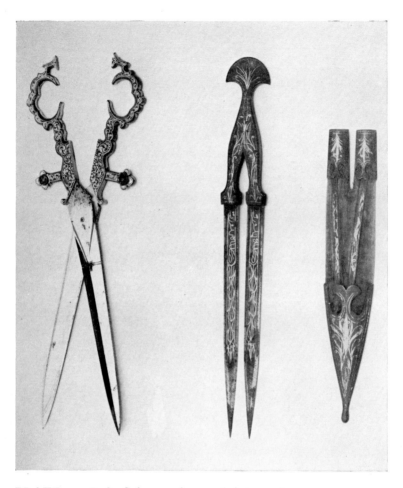

PLATE 195 *Left:* Scissors dagger (plate 194) open.
Right: Rather unusual fork dagger with sheath. Simple,
almost crude, silver inlay decorates sheath, blade and hilt.
Overall length $11\frac{3}{5}$ ins. Blades $7\frac{1}{10}$ ins.
Tunisian. 19th century.

INDEX

Plate numbers are shown in bold face type

Index

Index

Index

Index

Index